From Hollywood to Heaven

Steve Wohlberg

Pacific Press® Publishing Association
Nampa, Idaho
Oshawa, Ontario, Canada
www.pacificpress.com

PROPERTY OF CITY OF LOS ANGELES

D0728725

Copyright 2006 by
Pacific Press® Publishing Association
Printed in the United States of America
All rights reserved

Cover design by Mark Bond
Cover photo of Steve Wohlberg by Kristin Wohlberg
Inside design by Steve Lanto

Unless otherwise marked, Scripture quotations are from the NKJV, the Holy
Bible, The New King James Version, copyright © 1979, 1980, 1982 by Thomas
Nelson, Inc. Used by permission.
Scripture quotations marked RSV are from the Revised Standard Version of the
Bible, copyright © 1946, 1952, 1971, by the Division of Christian Education of
the National Council of the Churches of Christ in the U.S.A. Used by permission.
All rights reserved.

Library of Congress Cataloging-in-Publication Data

Wohlberg, Steve, 1959-
From Hollywood to heaven:
A riveting story of one man's journey from darkness into light.
p. cm.
ISBN: 0-8163-2145-0
ISBN 13: 9780816321452
1. Wohlberg, Steve, 1959- 2. Seventh-day Adventist converts—United States—
Biography. I. Title.
•
BX6189.W56A3 2006
286.7092—dc22
[B]
2005058693

You can contact Steve Wohlberg at White Horse Media,
P.O. Box 8057, Fresno, California 93747;
<www.whitehorsemedia.com>.

Additional copies of this book are available by calling toll free 1-800-765-6955 or
by visiting <www.adventistbookcenter.com>.

06 07 08 09 10 • 5 4 3 2 1

Dedication

To my mother, Sandy Wohlberg:
Mom, you have done so much for me.
I love you more than words can express!

To my wife, Kristin:
Thank God, I finally found you.
Your companionship is one of life's greatest treasures.

Other books by Steve Wohlberg

The Antichrist Chronicles

Truth Left Behind

Will My Pet Go to Heaven?

End Time Delusions

Hidden Dangers in Harry Potter

Hour of the Witch

Contents

*"Hollywood is a place where they'll pay you
fifty thousand dollars for a kiss and fifty cents for your soul."
~Marilyn Monroe (1926–1962),
American movie actress*

*"If God doesn't destroy Hollywood Boulevard,
He owes Sodom and Gomorrah an apology."
~Jay Leno (1950–),
American comedian and TV talk-show host*

Foreword

"For it is the God who commanded light to shine out of darkness
who has shone in our hearts."
—*2 Corinthians 4:6*

Throughout the past twenty-six years, I have told portions of my story during seminars and interviews, but I've persistently resisted a nagging impression to write it down. There are a couple of reasons: Much of my past isn't pleasant, and I haven't wanted to draw so much attention to myself. However, because many people have said they want to see my story in print and because I think it can help others, I've taken the plunge. In telling my story, I have left out many degenerate details because they wouldn't inspire anyone and wouldn't serve my purpose. But I'll tell you enough that you'll get the picture.

Hollywood isn't entirely evil; some scattered stars illuminate the night there. Yet anyone with half a conscience can see that far too many Hollywood movies, TV series, and musicians promote values that lead downward, toward slime and the pit, and away from common decency, goodness, and heaven. And while in many Hollywood movies, the heroes live "happily ever after," that's only on the screen. In real life, Hollywood stars may end up in prison or dead in some hotel room from an overdose of drugs. To be blunt, much of Hollywood corrupts and can kill. I know. It almost destroyed me.

As you read my story, you may relate to my confusion and struggles. You might even think that your life story resembles mine. You'll be pleased to know, then, that this book has a happy ending. If your life is anywhere near the edge or just empty and unfulfilled, you can still live happily ever after—for real. Heaven is a real place, and it's waiting for you. This book will help you get there.

1

Hollywood Hills

"Every life is a march from innocence,
through temptation, to virtue or vice."
~ Lyman Abbott (1835–1922),
American religious leader

Temple Hospital, Los Angeles, California, April 5, 1959—
"It's a boy!" the doctor exclaimed to Gene and Sandra Wohlberg.
Of course, I don't remember that moment, but I had arrived—a
healthy, wiggly, energetic baby. One year later, my brother, Michael, came along. Then, after six more years, our sister, Cathy,
joined us. I remember feeling Cathy's vigorous kicks inside
Mom's tummy before she emerged, which was very exciting to
me.

Six of us—Dad, Mom, me, Mike, Cathy, and Jackie Fowler,
Mom's sister—lived together at 3150 Donna Maria Drive, a corner house in a hilly neighborhood known as Laurelwood just west
of the famous Hollywood sign that overlooks LA's smoggy basin.
The larger community is called Studio City; it's named after nearby Universal Studios, where many movies are filmed and edited.
By meandering to the top of our hill and then down the other side

on Laurel Canyon Boulevard, one can easily reach Hollywood itself, the steamy Sunset Strip, or ritzy Beverly Hills.

The first twelve years of my life seemed normal, at least for a boy growing up in the shadows of the entertainment capital of the world. Like most kids, I started out on the innocent side of life. I rolled on skateboards with neighborhood friends, flipped basketballs into hoops across the street from our home, created a butterfly collection, and hiked in the Hollywood Hills catching lizards—I became an expert lizard catcher. I also accumulated lots of pets. At one point, our house and yard resembled a small zoo. We housed an extremely lovable Great Dane, a calico cat, rabbits, a chicken, a rooster, a bird, fish tanks, tadpoles, frogs, turtles, lizards, snakes, a hamster, and a foot-long alligator that I creatively named Ali. I remember one occasion on which the woman who cleaned our house poked her head inside the front door and shouted out before entering, "Steven, is anything loose?"

Some of my fondest childhood memories are of fishing trips with my dad and brother. Dad would quietly enter our bedroom at 4 A.M. and whisper, "OK, boys! Are you ready to go fishing?" We would awake in a flash and soon be on our way to Redondo Beach or San Diego to board fishing boats full of anglers hoping to catch bonito, barracuda, rock cod, or an occasional halibut. Once, Mike even won the jackpot for catching the biggest fish. We were two wide-eyed little boys happily carrying our fishing rods, fascinated by the rolling ocean, excited to wiggle anchovies onto our fishing hooks, eager to feel a nibble on our fishing line, oblivious to the world around us. We were thrilled just to spend time with our dad. We had lots of fun with Mom, too. Those times were great.

Our family was big into sports. At an early age, Mike and I joined the Studio City Little League, and soon our dad became our team coach. We also joined the Indian Guides (similar to Boy Scouts), went to summer camps, swam in swim meets, and joined a bowling league. After regular basketball, baseball, football, and bowling games, we usually went to the Sav-On Drug Store on Ventura Boulevard to devour double-scoop hot fudge sundaes. Like most kids, we ate lots of ice cream!

We also watched a lot of TV. On Saturday mornings, Mike and I sat fixated before cartoons, watching Road Runner, Daffy Duck, Yosemite Sam, Bugs Bunny, and Woody the Woodpecker. These seemed innocent enough. After school during the week, we switched the tube on again and soon became hooked on *Batman* and *Gilligan's Island.* And after dark, we watched *My Three Sons, Lone Ranger, Get Smart,* and *Bonanza.* It wasn't long, however, until I noticed that our *TV Guide* listed movies that weren't so family friendly, such as horror flicks about blood-sucking vampires, Frankenstein's monster, scary werewolves, and Egyptian mummies that returned to life to terrorize the living. By the time I was eight or nine years old, I was often up until 1 A.M., reclining on pillows, eating ice cream, and watching monster movies. Step by step, these shows introduced darker elements into my young mind. Hollywood was moving in.

As for religion, our home had very little. We were a Jewish family, to be sure; yet we didn't go to the synagogue. We had Jewish friends who lived across the street, and sometimes we went to their home for Passover Seders, to eat fruit, nuts, honey, matzo crackers, horseradish sauce, and portions of lamb. On Sunday mornings, we often walked down Laurel Canyon and visited Art's deli for traditional lox, cream cheese, and bagels. Mom and Aunt Jackie were great cooks, and we enjoyed Jewish food. However, my parents didn't keep a kosher home, so we ate just about anything, including ham, bacon, and salami. One thing I couldn't stomach was chopped liver. I always hated chopped liver!

At age twelve, Mike received his bar mitzvah—a ceremony that marks a Jewish boy's transition to manhood—in a synagogue in Studio City. It was a big occasion. I still remember my brother standing before the rabbi, the Torah (the first five books of Moses), and a host of family and friends as he respectfully recited Hebrew phrases. I had no clue what the words he said meant. After the service, we all went back to our house for food and fun, including a hired magician who performed magic tricks.

"Steve, do you want a bar mitzvah?" my dad asked me once. "I have nothing to urge," he said.

After thinking about how many ball games I might have to miss while I prepared for the ceremony, I said something like "Er . . . ah . . . not really," and that was that. So, while Mike learned Hebrew words, I played basketball, roamed the hills, and caught lizards.

I remember being vaguely curious about one Jewish custom. During the few Passover Seders we attended at the home of friends, the host family usually set an empty chair at the dinner table for someone named Elijah. Malachi 4:5 says, " 'Behold, I will send Eli'jah the prophet before the great and terrible day of the LORD comes' " (RSV). A Jewish tradition rooted in that verse speculates that the ancient prophet Elijah might return during the Passover to herald the arrival of the Messiah. The empty chair symbolizes Judaism's expectation that someday our Messiah will come. However, just as Elijah's chair was empty during those Passovers, so that expectation was absolutely empty for us. We never talked about any messiah or about God at all.

I appreciate my family, but something was missing. As far as I can remember, my family never once prayed at home. I don't think we even owned a Bible, never mind read from one. The main books I read as a child were from the Dr. Seuss series: *Green Eggs and Ham, Horton Hears a Who!* and *The Cat in the Hat Comes Back.* But mostly I watched monster movies produced in Hollywood studios. I had no thoughts of heaven. One day this would change dramatically.

2

Teenage Trouble

"Please allow me to introduce myself
I'm a man of wealth and taste
I've been around for a long, long year
Stole many a man's soul and faith . . .
Just call me Lucifer."
~ Lyrics from The Rolling Stones' hit song
"Sympathy for the Devil"

Music became a molding force in my life, influencing me in the wrong direction. As with my TV viewing, the music I listened to at first was mild, my favorite songs being ones such as "Precious and Few," "Could It Be I'm Falling in Love," "Time in a Bottle" (Aunt Jackie loved Jim Croce), "Basketball Jones," and "The Lion Sleeps Tonight." In the 1960s, the Beatles became big, and I was soon singing their songs too—musical numbers such as "I Want to Hold Your Hand," "A Hard Day's Night," "Yellow Submarine," and "Lucy in the Sky With Diamonds." Step by step, song by song, album by album, these songs and others like them introduced me to the world of rock and roll—and to the values the singers were promoting.

While the Beatles themselves started out semimild, it's no secret that they became heavy drug users. I had no idea that the repetitious lyrics of one of their hit songs, "Smokes pot, smokes pot, everybody smokes pot" would soon be true of me too. But that's what happened. The old adage "Monkey see, monkey do" still holds true. Whether we like it or not, what we watch, read, and listen to does affect us. Slowly but surely, we become what we tune into. Unknown to me, Hollywood had started transforming me into its image.

As I entered my teens in the 1970s, I still enjoyed basketball, hiking, swimming, and fishing. But my music grew louder, and the songs became crazier. Gradually, I shifted from soft-rock groups such as the Monkeys and the Beatles to harder tunes emanating from noisier bands such as Aerosmith, Black Sabbath, Tubes, Led Zeppelin, and The Rolling Stones. The same Jewish boy who enjoyed Dr. Seuss books and curiously watched his brother's bar mitzvah now found himself surrounded by a group of teenage buddies increasingly attracted to every element in the popular slogan "sex, drugs, and rock 'n' roll." Without realizing it, we had become easy targets for temptation; we'd set our feet on a fast-moving "highway to hell," the very title of a rock album we listened to.

For me, temptation struck hard in the back of a school bus early one morning as I was being driven to Walter Reed Junior High. A blond girlfriend of mine who lived around the corner from me and whose parents my family knew well (her father was an actor, her mother a comedian) lit a cigarettelike object and passed it to me. "Take a toke, Steve; you'll like it," she said with a sweet smile. Not wanting to seem weird or straight-laced, I took my first puff of marijuana. This tiny event marked the beginning of six years of drug use that could easily have cost me my life. I was fourteen years old and in ninth grade.

If you asked me at that time, I would have said I belonged to a normal, happy family. Yet two years later, my parents entered my room and stoically announced they were getting a divorce. "Do you want to live with Mom or Dad?" they asked. "With Dad," I mumbled without much thought. I still remember their comments about how maturely I was handling everything. Honestly, it wasn't maturity. I was just a sixteen-year-old kid who liked the idea of rooming with Dad.

In 1975, after the divorce was finalized, my parents sold our house in the hills, and we all moved down into the surrounding San Fernando Valley. Mike, Cathy, and my mother moved into a nice apartment on Balboa Boulevard in Encino, and my father and I moved into another apartment complex on the corner of Colfax and Burbank Boulevard, within easy walking distance of North Hollywood High School. (Aunt Jackie moved into her own apartment in nearby Burbank.)

I remember strolling for the first time with my father into the lobby of Club California Apartments to check out our new living arrangements. The complex had a pool, Jacuzzi, pool table, exercise room, and tennis court. *Cool!* I thought. *This is going to be fantastic.* You might think I'd have been experiencing some sort of deep-seated anger, resentment, confusion, or emotional pain because of the divorce. Many children do, but I didn't. Had Hollywood influenced me? I think so, for by that time I'd watched countless movies and TV shows that portrayed men and women casually having sex outside of marriage without worrying about consequences. Even in the 1970s, this was normal prime-time stuff. "If it feels good, do it" was the slogan of the age, and this became my unconscious philosophy also.

In many ways, the kid who skipped his bar mitzvah had now become a typical Hollywood teen: hardhearted, self-absorbed, without much of a conscience, and quite unaware of his surroundings. At that time, I had no conscious or subconscious longings for God or heaven. And I certainly wasn't searching for anything grand such as "truth," "meaning," or "purpose." Sorry; I just wasn't. Helping others? Doing something worthwhile with my life? Such thoughts never entered my teenage brain. Basketball, fishing, rock music, and girls—these were what interested me. Definitely girls.

From 1975 to 1977, I attended North Hollywood High School while living with my dad at Club California. During those risky days, I plunged deeper into drugs and wild living. (Somehow I passed all my classes, though I skipped school a lot.) My friends and I, considering ourselves indestructible, attended sleazy parties in the Hollywood Hills, smoked pot at rock concerts throughout the LA area, and frequented nightclubs like Dillons, Starwood, Whiskey, and Odyssey around Hollywood and the Strip.

In the late 1970s, disco dancing became the rave, and my favorite movie was *Saturday Night Fever,* starring John Travolta and featuring his hit song "Disco Inferno." In the words of the Boston *Globe,* that movie was "Glitter. Glam. Disco. Trash. Travolta. Disco! Pop. Pap. Polyester. Innocuous. Immoral. Enervating." Casting off all restraint, my pals and I danced to the beat and burned all right, just as Travolta's song said. We burned with lust over every sexy sweetheart swaying nearby. And moving beyond marijuana, we progressed to harder drugs, including cocaine, LSD, and angel dust. We thought it was all fun and games—just Hollywood magic. But it wasn't. I remember how shocked I was to learn that one of our high school friends overdosed one night. Doctors couldn't revive her, and she died. It's a miracle I'm not six feet under the ground in some cemetery like poor Lisa.

One night, my friend John and I attended a rock concert in Los Angeles. As usual, we used drugs and drank heavily. About two o'clock in the morning, we headed toward our homes in

North Hollywood. I was driving. I still remember pulling into a parking lot at about 3 A.M. and wondering where in the world we were. Looking hazily through the windshield, we saw a stretch of sand and heard waves crashing. "We're at the beach!" we gasped, realizing how far from home we were. In an alcohol- and drug-induced mental fog, I had turned onto the wrong freeway and driven west into Santa Monica. We sat there for a few moments, chuckled a bit, and headed north again. Only God knows how we made it home that night without crashing and killing ourselves.

During those aimless days attending North Hollywood High, I met Walter, a fellow student who soon came to live with Dad and me at Club California. Walter grew up in Colombia, South America, and his mother still lived in Bogotá, the capital city.

One summer, Walter decided to make a three-week trip to visit his mom, and he invited me along.

"Can I go?" I begged my dad.

"Sure; why not?" he casually responded.

My dad bought our tickets and wished us well, and we boarded an airplane at the Los Angeles airport. We didn't know it then, but this little pleasure excursion would become a very dangerous trip and cost Walter what little sanity he had left.

No one searched us for drugs at any airport en route to Bogotá, and we mistakenly assumed we wouldn't have much trouble picking some up while we were there and bringing them back. So, upon arriving in Colombia, Walter contacted some old buddies, and we bought quite a bit of marijuana and cocaine.

After staying in Bogotá for a week or so, we decided to take a bus north to visit Walter's aunt in the city of Barranquilla. Our itinerary took us from Bogotá through Medellín, a major drug center, and Cartagena into Barranquilla. We would return to Bogotá through Santa Marta. We took our drugs with us, stuffing them into the pockets of a pair of blue jeans, which we rolled up and placed inside our suitcase. The suitcase, then, was stowed with other luggage on top of the bus.

Around midnight as we were traveling toward Barranquilla, we awoke to find our bus unexpectedly pulling into a police station. Everyone was ushered outside, and we were shocked to see a group of uniformed officers with flashlights climb on top of our bus to search through the luggage! Fear gripped us. *If they find our stuff, should I run?* I wondered. Silently surveying the area, I soon realized we were in the middle of nowhere. In the eerie illumination cast by the taillights of our idling bus, I watched a large tarantula spider creep across the dusty road toward an open field. *There's nowhere to go,* I concluded. Fortunately, the officers didn't find anything, and we were soon bumping along again.

At about 5 A.M., we arrived at the depot of a small town near our destination. Walter and I left the bus, grabbed our suitcase, and headed down the road toward his aunt's house. Suddenly, a small police car screeched up to the curb, and four men jumped out. *"Policía!"* they shouted. They grabbed our suitcase, threw it down, unzipped it, and began another search. My heart almost skipped a beat as I saw one officer grab the pair of rolled up jeans in which we had hidden our drugs. But he threw them aside without unrolling them. Finding nothing unusual, the four men grunted and sped away, leaving our belongings scattered on the sidewalk. Walter and I stared at each other in disbelief. Two close calls in one day!

We arrived at the home of Walter's aunt safe and sound. She hadn't seen Walter in many years, and they had a pleasant reunion. Her home was small and simple, and I was fascinated to see tiny geckos, one of my favorite kinds of lizards, clutching the walls and ceilings. Walter and I caught up on our sleep and ate tasty Colombian food.

The next night, we decided to stroll around town in search of a secluded spot where we could smoke some of our marijuana. We found a baseball diamond near a field of trees and entered the brush, where we assumed no one would see us. Sitting down in a clearing lit by moonlight, we were about to take out our drugs, when a lone police officer holding a flashlight and a rifle unexpectedly emerged from behind a tree! Walter conversed briefly with him in Spanish, and then the man walked away. We immediately left the field thinking, *This is unbelievable—three close calls in two days!*

Our three-week stint in South America passed quickly, and the time finally came for us to fly back to the United States. Walter still had some unfinished business to attend to. He had loaned his backpack to a friend, who hadn't yet returned it. So, Walter decided to stay a few extra days before coming home.

We discussed whether I should take some of the drugs we had purchased in Bogotá back to the States. Would I be searched? Probably not, we reasoned, because no one had searched us en route to South America. But just to be on the safe side, we sat down just outside the airport and snorted our last bit of cocaine. Walter kept the marijuana, and I took nothing. Inside the airport, we parted at a security checkpoint.

"See ya in a few days."

"Right!"

"Bye for now."

How wrong we were.

At that point, I was without a translator in a country whose language I didn't speak. As I approached a second checkpoint, I was stunned when a police officer suddenly grabbed my shoulder and motioned for me to follow him. He led me into a small room where the luggage from the first checkpoint was stacked, and he muttered some phrases I couldn't understand. Eventually, I figured out that he wanted me to identify my suitcase, which was at the bottom of the stack. "That one," I said, pointing. "That's mine."

A couple of men pulled it out and searched it thoroughly. They also made me strip off all my clothes except my undershorts. "Nada," they said, scowling, as I watched in utter amazement. *Wow, that was close!* I thought.

After dressing again, I was ushered back to a line of people close to the gate from which my plane was scheduled to depart. Then I noticed a clock on the wall. Only a few minutes remained until my flight would leave, yet one more checkpoint stood between America and me. A security guard stopped me, muttering something in half-broken English.

"Look! My plane is about to leave. I need to go!" I pleaded.

He stuttered back something like, "If you miss flight, you go tomorrow."

In desperation, I looked at his nametag, pointed my finger at him, and barked, "YOU, MR. GOMEZ [or whatever his name was], MY PAPA IN AMERICA IS VERY IMPORTANT! IF I AM NOT ON THAT PLANE, YOU ARE IN BIG TROUBLE! LET ME GO NOW!"

The guard's eyes widened, he motioned *Go,* and I ran down the corridor as fast as I could, entering the plane just moments before the door slammed shut.

When I landed in Los Angeles and set my feet on U.S. soil, I was happier to be in America than I had ever been before in my entire life! "How was your trip?" my dad asked innocently at the gate.

"Oh, fine. Walter's mother is nice. He decided to stay a few extra days to retrieve a backpack he loaned to a friend. He'll come back next week."

"OK," my father replied as we walked arm in arm toward our car.

Whew, I thought many times as we drove out of the airport, up

Interstate 405, into the San Fernando Valley, and back to our apartment in North Hollywood with its tennis court, pool, and Jacuzzi.

The next day, Walter's mother phoned from Bogotá and informed us that Walter had been thrown into a Colombian prison after a passing police officer on the street unexpectedly searched him and found a bag of marijuana stashed inside his sock. "Please, help me!" she pleaded desperately.

We tried. My dad spent lots of money trying to get Walter out of jail, but a number of times right after he sent money, we were notified that Walter had been transferred to another prison. After many weeks of expensive suspense, Walter was finally released and allowed to return to America.

But he wasn't the same person. I shudder to think what he endured inside the dingy chambers of those Colombian jails. Whatever had happened had caused his mind to crack. A few months later, I visited him at a San Fernando Valley facility for the mentally ill. Poor Walter.

Right around that time, I saw a frightening film titled *Midnight Express*. This film was based on a true story about an American tourist named William Hayes who was arrested in South America for drug trafficking and who spent many years behind bars. After horrible experiences, Hayes finally escaped. Watching that film, I realized what could easily have happened to me. It terrified me. I had blondish hair, lightened by sunny days at the beach. If I had been thrown into a Colombian prison, I probably never would have gotten out.

How did I survive those crazy days? I don't know. Some of my other friends didn't make it. I already told you about Lisa. Another friend of mine, Michael, an athlete who visited our Club Cal apartments many times, died of liver disease because he poured too much alcohol into his body. In the midst of all my foolishness, Someone must have been looking out for me.

* * *

There it stood, right off Highway 170, straight across from the famous Hollywood Bowl, on a hill by itself. I passed it many times while driving from Studio City into Hollywood. It was a large cross, yet I hardly noticed. Each evening it lit up and shed its illuminating rays toward dark street corners where hookers and pimps earned dismal dollars preying on lost souls seeking forbidden pleasures. Hollywood pleasantly attracts, temptingly invites, and then sucks people in until they can't escape. Yet the cross remains. Even today, its light still shines above Glitterland.

Though I, an out-of-control teenager, didn't realize it at the time, an amazing sequence of events was about to kick into motion what would finally open my blind eyes to the message of hope that the cross represents.

Someone loved me.

He had a plan for my life.

Close Encounters of the Spiritual Kind

"Chance is a nickname for Providence."
~ Sebastien Roch Nicolas Chamfort (1741–1794),
French writer

As far as I recall, it all started one lazy afternoon as John and I made our way to a favorite trout stream forty-five minutes north of Los Angeles. John, a good friend of mine, and I often headed up Interstate 5 past Magic Mountain and Lake Castaic to Templin Canyon and a narrow mountain road that zigzagged toward a creek that ran out of the backside of Lake Pyramid. We loved that little stream. Sometimes we went just for the day; other times we loaded our backpacks and spent the weekend. John and I had a lot in common. We both liked basketball, disco dancing, chasing girls, and trout fishing. We also smoked lots of marijuana together almost every time we went to the mountains.

This particular time, as usual, I drove. I parked the car at the end of Templin Canyon, and we grabbed our fishing poles and night crawlers and began our journey deep into the winding mountain switchbacks, away from people and toward isolated water holes that contained more fish. I don't remember how long we'd been hiking, perhaps an hour, when I glanced up toward a steep slope and saw a strange set of words painted on the face of a large rock. Someone must have climbed up there with a spray gun. There were three words: "Repent or perish."

I was nineteen years old and had never walked into a church in my life. *Heaven, God, the Bible*—I hardly knew what those words meant. Suddenly, however, "repent or perish" assaulted my leisurely trek. I vaguely remember that those ominous words startled me and that for a few seconds I tried to figure out what they meant. Something told me that whatever they meant was serious. Then I thought, *Oh well, so much for that. Back to fishing.* Yet somewhere deep within, those three little words stuck with me. Seed number one had just been planted into my teenage brain.

A little later, I landed a job at Longs Drug Store, located right on the corner of Hollywood Boulevard and Highland Avenue. Even today, this intersection is world famous. It's close to the Hollywood Wax Museum, Grauman's Chinese Theatre, and the Avenue of the Stars, which contains the footprints of Glitterland's hottest celebrities. My job wasn't so glamorous. I was only a stock boy, responsible for placing merchandise on the shelves. The pay was minimum wage.

"Steve, will you walk down the street and pick up something for me?" my boss asked one day.

"Sure!" I said, and I was out the door in a flash. As I casually strolled down Hollywood Boulevard, minding my own business, suddenly I felt a tug on my sleeve. Turning around, I saw a young girl, about fourteen years old, holding a Bible.

"Yes? What?" I asked.

"Excuse me, sir. Are you saved?" she asked kindly, but forcibly.

If a hidden camera had caught the expression on my face, it would have revealed a look of total bewilderment. My exact response was, "Saved? I didn't know I was lost!"

It's true. I didn't.

That concluded our brief conversation. I walked away dumbfounded and returned to my boss at Longs Drug Store. Although I didn't realize it, however, the girl followed me.

Back inside the store, I returned to my task of placing toothpaste and dental floss on shelves. A short time later, I glanced to my left and was shocked to see that same girl peeking around one of aisles and staring at me! *Oh no,* I thought. *There's that Bible girl. She's following me!*

When our eyes met, the girl snapped her head back behind the shelves and vanished. I never saw her again. *How weird!* I thought. *What was that all about?* I had no clue then and still don't to this day. However, another spiritual seed had been planted inside my head by an unknown, Bible-carrying girl who asked me, "Sir, are you saved?"

Another event took place that startled my carefree young life—this time in Palm Springs. My buddies and I frequently made the two-hour drive there from Los Angeles on Interstate 10 to cruise the desert's main drag, Highway 111, hoping to meet girls. The boulevard was particularly packed with reckless teens during our school's spring break, usually in March. One Saturday night, a group of us were casually walking down Highway 111, passing under palm trees and eating ice cream, when we noticed an odd sight. Two young men were standing in the back of a pickup truck and, with the aid of megaphones, were preaching about God to the jostling crowd.

I have no idea why I did it, but I thoughtlessly shouted, "Hey, I'm an atheist!" toward the guys in the pickup. Did I know what an atheist was? Nope. The words just rolled out of my impetuous mouth. Unexpectedly, one of the men in the truck heard me, leveled his megaphone directly toward my head, and shouted back something like, "Hey you—you're a fool! When the day of judgment arrives, you'll be on the wrong side."

I almost swallowed my tongue. The force of that man's high-decibel response jolted my complacency and actually produced fear in my heart. I stood silenced—stunned and rebuked. *Fool? Day of judgment? Wrong side?* These weren't pleasant thoughts to my cocaine-clouded brain. Really now, I had driven to Palm Springs to find girls, not God, and thinking about Him was about as foreign to me as evolution is to a creationist. It wasn't part of my universe. I don't remember how long the impression lasted—not long, I'm sure. Nevertheless, it was there, having suddenly invaded the head of an irreligious teenager. *Day of judgment?* Scary thought!

There were numerous spots that my friends and I liked to frequent. In addition to Palm Springs, Van Nuys Boulevard, Hollywood Boulevard, and the Strip, there was the exciting town of Westwood, in the shadow of UCLA. Westwood was filled with movie theaters, discos, ice-cream parlors, street performers, celebrities, and of course, lots of teenage girls. It's amazing that any serious spiritual impressions can be made in such a noisy, crazy environment, but they can. God works there, too, even though His presence isn't usually sought or welcomed.

I still remember the moment. One Friday or Saturday night, my actor-dancer-singer-writer friend, Steve, and I were walking around Westwood when a young man approached us carrying an old, tattered Bible. He was witnessing for Jesus Christ, just like the Bible girl who tugged my sleeve on Hollywood Boulevard. Steve was friendly, and he struck up a conversation with the stranger, while I stood motionless, listening. I remember how earnest that boy looked. His face expressed deep interest, compassion, and concern as he talked about Noah, the Flood, and the approaching end of the world. His eyes were intense, yet loving.

At that time in my life, this guy seemed like some sort of alien in a Star Wars flick, very different from anyone I knew. Near the end of the conversation, he turned to me and asked for my phone number. "Can I call you sometime and invite you to church?"

"Me? Well . . . er . . . OK, here's my number."

I gave it to him, and then he disappeared into the crowd.

Three years after my parents' divorce, my dad married a woman named Anne Brookes, and the three of us moved into a three-story condominium in Studio City, not far from North Hollywood High. My bedroom was on the lower level, and what a room it was! Black-light posters lined my walls, a mirror spanned the ceiling, a big waterbed sat in the center, a king-size yellow beanbag chair leaned against a wall, and a strobe light flashed psychedelic colors everywhere at night.

This room was much "cooler" than my former room in Burbank, and it quickly became a popular hangout, where my friends and I puffed marijuana laced with honey oil through bamboo tubes called "bongs," lined cocaine with razor blades on mirrors before snorting it up our noses, guzzled beer, and listened to rock groups like Led Zeppelin, ZZ Top, Aerosmith, and Blue Oyster Cult. I think I stayed healthy only because I danced for hours in discothèques and played lots of basketball. These activities gave me some great workouts.

Ring . . . ring . . . ring.

"Hello?" I casually breathed into the phone in my bedroom. "Who? Oh, . . . you." It was the man Steve and I had met in Westwood. I vaguely recalled giving him my phone number; now he was inviting me to visit his church. I don't remember the details of that conversation except that it was short and that I never went to church with him. I do remember how bizarre the whole thing seemed. Who were these people who carried Bibles and talked about God? *Strange, very strange,* I thought. Then I forgot about it.

Sometime later, I went dancing at a club called the Starwood on the corner of Highland Avenue and Santa Monica Boulevard, not far from Vine Street, where transvestites and drag queens hung out. It was a dingy part of town. The relentless beat of disco music along with the pungent odors of tobacco and liquor assaulted my ears and nose. I didn't mind, though. In fact, I enjoyed it.

That particular night I met a dark-haired girl about my age, and the two of us eventually left the club and stopped at a Denny's restaurant for a snack. It was about 4 A.M. As we sat at a table and talked, my "date" unexpectedly introduced a new topic. "Steve," she said, "you won't believe what I saw at a party the other night!"

My eyes widened a bit. "What?" I asked.

I still remember gazing into her dark eyes as she continued. "There I was, sitting in a large room, just curiously watching people, when I noticed across the room a woman surrounded by men. She was drinking, smoking, acting sleazy, and she intrigued me. As I watched this lady with interest, suddenly, something *very strange* happened. It was like my eyes were opened and I saw an invisible world become visible. Shadowy, dark forms appeared all around that woman, floating in a circle. They looked evil, *very evil*. I was terrified. I think I saw the devil!"

I placed my Coke on the table, stunned. "You think you saw the devil?" I repeated.

Believe it or not, this was one of the first times anyone had ever told me anything about a devil. Of course, if you had shown me a picture of a reddish being with two horns and a pitchfork, I would have said, "That's the devil." One Halloween when I was a kid, I wore a devil costume. Then there were those Red Devil fireworks that we set off every Fourth of July. But that was all fun and fiction. No one had ever told me there was a *real devil,* much less that they had seen him or his demons. But that's what this girl said.

I don't remember the girl's name, and I never saw her again, but her strange story stuck with me. *A party, a sleazy woman, the invisible world, the devil. . . . Hmm, very interesting.* I wasn't conscious of it, but something new started growing inside me. I still used drugs, guzzled beer, went to rock concerts, cranked up my stereo, and acted crazy, but a sleepy part of my head was stirring. My conscience was waking up. "Repent or perish." "Sir, are you saved?" "You fool, . . . the wrong side on the day of judgment." "Will you come to church with me?" and "I think I saw the devil!" All of these apparently disconnected and isolated events penetrated my spiritual deadness.

And although I didn't realize it, this was just the beginning . . .

4

The Summer
of '79

"The Creator of the universe works in mysterious ways."
~ *Scott Raymond Adams (1957–),*
American cartoonist

During my teen years, I couldn't hold a steady job for more than a few months. I went door to door for a carpet company in the San Fernando Valley, worked at a tropical fish store in Studio City, sold Shaklee vitamins, sorted receipts for a tax attorney in Hollywood, stocked shelves at Longs Drug Store, and swept floors at Mother Nature's Health Food Store in North Hollywood. None of these jobs required much skill, and I had no vocational training anyway.

Overall, my life was happy-go-lucky. My father worked hard, made good money as co-owner of a carpet business in West Hollywood, provided for our family, bought my first car, paid for my education, and gave me pretty much whatever I asked for. My dad is a kind man and very generous, but he'll be the first to admit that during that time he didn't impart much morality to me. In fact, I don't think he ever disciplined me! One time I mistakenly left a bag of marijuana right on his bed, not retrieving it until sometime later. He couldn't have missed it, but he never said a word.

After my dad married Anne, the three of us lived in their Studio City condo for about two years (1977–1979) while I attended Los Angeles Valley College, taking general education classes. I had no clue what I wanted to be when I "grew up." My life was perfectly directionless, composed mostly of fishing excursions into the mountains north of LA, backpacking with my friend John, playing basketball, sun tanning on beaches, going to movies, cruising around Hollywood, smoking pot, snorting cocaine, going to wild parties, and disco dancing. But after my twentieth birthday, I sensed the nagging need to get my rear into gear and choose a career. After all, I couldn't live with Dad forever, and if I was going to maintain any kind of enjoyable lifestyle, I needed to start thinking seriously about landing a permanent job and making some real money.

"Any suggestions on where I might work this summer?" I asked my dad one lazy spring day. Unexpectedly, he had one. The lyrics of an old song say, "Slip out the back, Jack." Sound familiar? Well, my father knew that very Jack, and Jack had connections in the entertainment industry. Pulling a few strings, he lined up a job for me working as an extra in Hollywood movies. In TV shows and movies, actors act and extras fill backgrounds. Extras are the crowd, the no-names. They have no real connection to the storyline other than standing around to make scenes look real. Because my dad knew Jack, and because Jack knew so-and-so, after I graduated from Los Angeles Valley College, I was officially accepted into the Screen Extras Guild and entered show business. It was the summer of '79. *This is super cool!* were my exact thoughts.

I was instructed to drive over the hill from Studio City into Hollywood to a slick building leased by the Central Casting Agency just beyond the Sunset Strip, on the edge of Beverly

Hills. I found the building, parked my car, went inside, gave my name at the front desk, and was quickly ushered into a private room to be eyeballed, analyzed, and interviewed about my "skills." Twenty years old, six feet tall, one hundred and fifty-five pounds, blondish hair, hazel eyes, et cetera. "I dance, play basketball, am a pretty good athlete, and can do just about whatever you want," I told the agency. Because Jack was my dad's friend, I got in.

A few days later—after my bio registered in their system—I called the casting agency and asked if they had any work for me. "Steve Wohlberg. . . . Let's see. . . . Yes, we do," was the reply I heard—and kept hearing for the next three months. They sent me to various studios or filming sites "on location." Throughout that summer, I showed up at Burbank Studios, Universal Studios, Walt Disney Studios, and Paramount Studios for tiny parts in various movies, commercials, and TV shows like *The Bad News Bears, The Waltons, Boy Meets Girl, Family,* and *Eleventh Victim,* which was about California's infamous Hillside Strangler. I danced, slurped Coca Cola in a malt shop, drove a truck onto a military base, sat on a sexy woman's lap in a nightclub, and posed as a hitchhiker eerily eyed by the strangler. None of these tasks took any real talent. *Big deal,* I thought. *Hey, I'm in the movies!*

Then it happened—a day destined to alter the course of my entire life.

"Hi, I'm Steve Wohlberg," I notified the operator at Central Casting. "Do you have any work for me today?"

"Hold on. . . . Yes, your assignment is on location at Oxnard Beach. You'll have a small part in a mini-series based on a film called *From Here to Eternity.*"

The title sounded good, but it didn't particularly register with me. However, though I didn't realize it at the time, the title of that movie would become prophetic. The "one small step" I would be taking onto Oxnard Beach would become for me "one giant leap" toward eternity! I cranked up my car stereo while pulling away from our home in Studio City, drove forty-five minutes to sunny Oxnard Beach, just north of Malibu, and reported for duty.

Upon arrival, I discovered my role was to wear an army outfit, grip a rifle, and sprint across the sand during a battle scene. Filming movie scenes often requires multiple "takes" before the director is satisfied with the segment. In between takes, the actors and extras lounge around, sip coffee, play cards, and twiddle their thumbs.

We sat around a lot that day. The rolling waves of the Pacific Ocean rhythmically surged forward and backward while we relaxed on the sand, and the sea air was fresh—it was a perfect California day. Sometime before noon, as a few other extras and I were talking, playing cards, and smoothing on suntan lotion, another extra approached us. This man was a Christian, and he had decided to use his downtime to share his faith. "How are you guys?" he asked as we shuffled our playing cards.

"Just fine; how about you?" we thoughtlessly responded.

I don't remember this fellow extra's exact words, but after some chitchat, he began talking about biblical prophecies and the end of the world. Just like that girl on Hollywood Boulevard and the man in Westwood, he spoke earnestly about the Bible and his beliefs. The rest of our little group didn't appear impressed or even remotely interested in being "saved" that day, but my curiosity was piqued. For the first time ever, I wanted to hear more—I guess all those tiny seeds previously tossed into the soil of my mind were sprouting. So, during the noon hour, while a catering truck provided hot dogs and pizza to our film crew, I sought this man out, sat beside him, and we ate lunch together.

"What's this about the end of the world?" I asked him. "Are you serious?"

With the ocean waves pounding Oxnard's sandy shore just a few yards away, this young man proceeded to tell me about his personal faith in God and what the Bible predicted about the end of days. He also said there was a real entity named Satan who was operating invisibly behind the scenes, and he told me that this diabolical spirit was the hidden source of every problem on planet Earth. This intrigued me. I remembered that woman at the Denny's restaurant who claimed she had seen the devil. *Hmm,* I remember thinking. *Here I am, working behind the scenes in the movies. Perhaps there are other things going on behind the scenes that the world isn't aware of.* This thought made a distinct impression on me.

Near the end of our meal, this man challenged me. "If you want to know what's happening," he said, "you need to get a Bible and some good prophecy books and start reading."

Why not? I thought to myself. *It's time to check this out.* So, when the director was satisfied with our sandy scenes, I left Oxnard Beach determined to find a Bible.

I remembered that my stepmother had been raised a Southern Baptist. *Maybe Anne has a copy lying around,* I thought. So, when I arrived back at our condominium, I checked the bookshelf in the den upstairs—and, lo and behold, there was an old black Book sitting on the shelf. I still remember slowly reaching out and grabbing that ancient volume. This was the first time my fingers—so used to holding beer cans and striking matches—ever touched something sacred.

The next day I phoned Central Casting looking for more work. I was instructed to drive to a Los Angeles school building for some on-location filming for a show called *Family,* which featured child-actress Kristy McNichol. Imagining I would have plenty of time to kill between takes, I took the Bible with me. After arriving at the school and shooting a few scenes, the expected let's-twiddle-our-thumbs moment came. So, I took out the

Bible, opened it, and curiously surveyed the table of contents. "Genesis, Exodus, Leviticus, Numbers, Deuteronomy, First Kings, Second Kings, Psalms, Proverbs . . ." These unfamiliar titles seemed weird to me.

"Ecclesiastes."

Ecclesiwhat? My eyes stopped there. *What a funny name. I wonder what it's about?*

Flipping pages, I located the twelve-chapter book and started reading about King Solomon, who was surrounded by wealth, wine, women, and song, but who discovered—when the titillating pleasures of sex and liquor wore off—that the whole thing was nothing more than "vanity and grasping for the wind" (Ecclesiastes 1:14). Despite all those pleasures, he found himself empty and unfulfilled.

In those days, one of my favorite songs contained the line, "I can't get no satisfaction," sung by Mick Jagger of The Rolling Stones. My buddies and I loved this song. In fact, we played it over and over again inside the home of our rich friend Kelly Campbell, daughter of country singer Glenn Campbell, when we visited the mansion Kelly lived in above the Hollywood Hills. In spite of Jagger's money—and he had tons of it—he found no real satisfaction in wild living. Neither had King Solomon.

Ecclesiastes, the first Bible book I ever read, was just what I needed. When I read that Solomon's money produced only "vanity and grasping for the wind," something mysterious happened. For the first time in my life, I sensed a strange, indefinable hole inside my heart. I hadn't really felt this before. Oddly enough, *reading the Book had produced that hole!* Yes, I was in show business. Yes, Hollywood celebrities and gorgeous women surrounded me. Yes, I had a fast car and cool friends. But something was missing. What was it? Could it be God?

"What are you reading?" an African-American stranger inquired, interrupting my chain of thought.

"Err . . . ah . . . it's a Bible," I replied, somewhat startled.

"Find anything interesting?" he continued.

"Well, yes," I commented a bit sheepishly. "Have you ever read this Book?"

Come to find out he had, for he was a young pastor training for the ministry. He wasn't part of our film crew, and the sight of a twenty-year-old reading a Bible offstage had caught his eye.

"I'm Michael," he said warmly, stretching out his hand.

"I'm Steve Wohlberg, one of the extras in this TV show."

After we talked for a while, Michael asked if I would be willing to visit his church some Sunday morning. This was the second time someone had invited me to visit a Christian church. I had turned the first offer down, but now I was ready to try it. "Sure, why not?" I said.

"Great," Michael happily responded. Scratching his phone number on a piece of paper, he said, "Call me soon, OK?" and then he walked away.

A few days later, I did just that, and the following Sunday morning I found myself driving from Studio City back into Los Angeles, searching for Slausen Avenue. I was about to discover a high-spirited black Baptist church. Everyone in the church soon noticed this twenty-year-old white Jewish kid. My circle of friends had no prejudice, and these people certainly didn't either.

Michael not only participated in the service but also introduced me to Pastor Harper, the senior minister. Imagine my shock when Pastor Harper led me to the front of the church, clasped my hands, and introduced me to his entire congregation! "This young man wants to know the Lord!" he enthusiastically declared.

"Amen!" shouted back the congregation.

"He wants to know Jesus!"

"Amen!" replied a chorus of voices.

This was my first experience inside a Christian church. It was an event I won't easily forget!

Returning to Studio City, I thought hard about everything that had occurred that day. Deep within, a struggle was brewing. Let me make this clear: At this point, I was certainly no Christian. Far from it—Hollywood was my name, and partying was still very much my game. In fact, I would continue drinking Coors, smoking pot, and snorting white powder for months. But new thoughts swirled around inside my nonreligious heart. As that California summer wore on, and as I drove back and forth to movie studios and film sites, I continued carrying my stepmother's black Bible to work so I could read it offstage in between takes. Ecclesiastes. Proverbs. Psalms. Isaiah. . . . It all started with *From Here to Eternity.*

The Voice in the Book grew stronger. But so did an opposing force that was unwilling to let me go.

5

The War
Within

"Conscience is the inner voice
that warns us somebody is looking."
~ H. L. Mencken (1880–1956),
American writer and critic

My teenage years were mostly carefree—one continual round of school, sports, hanging out with friends, beach trips, swimming, rock music, disco dancing, going to movies, backpacking, camping, fishing, hiking, parties, drugs, wine, and women. As I said before, during those days I didn't have a spiritual bone in my body, and I wasn't searching for any "higher power" or "greater good." God? Who was He—or she? Eternity? So what? I had absolutely no interest in the subject. None. Zip. Zero. I lived for *now.* Having fun was all that mattered.

That is, until those strange and initially unwelcome encounters with a few Bible believers injected new thoughts into my head, like tiny seeds planted in the soil of my soul. During the summer of '79, after meeting that fellow extra on the beach, then finding my stepmother's Bible, then meeting Michael, and then visiting the Baptist church in downtown LA, new questions surfaced. A struggle began.

When I was sitting offstage and reading the Bible, my eyes soon fell upon verses like, " 'God shall judge the righteous and the wicked, for there shall be a time there for every purpose and for every work' " (Ecclesiastes 3:17).

Ouch—a day of judgment? I blinked and cringed.

Again, I read, "Rejoice, O young man, in your youth, and let your heart cheer you in the days of your youth; walk in the ways of your heart, . . . but know that for all these God will bring you into judgment" (Ecclesiastes 11:9).

Bring *me* into judgment? Not a pleasant thought.

Solomon gave his book this startling ending: "Let us hear the conclusion of the whole matter: Fear God, and keep His commandments, for this is the whole duty of man. For God will bring every work into judgment, including every secret thing, whether it is good or it is evil" (Ecclesiastes 12:13, 14).

I understood these verses only dimly, but ominous impressions intruded into my reckless young life. I'm ashamed to admit it, but during those days my feet often wandered into nasty places around Hollywood and the Sunset Strip. With foolish naivety, I involved myself in things that could easily have resulted in a knife in my back and my body being found crumpled in some back alley. One night I was about to purchase what I thought was cocaine from a well-dressed stranger, when I realized the stuff was fake. Sitting beside me in my own car, this smooth-talking man shuffled his hand under his coat, said he had a gun, and threatened to kill me if I didn't pay up. I handed him a hundred bucks. Believe it or not, he then wanted to have sex with me, but I talked my way out before anything happened. This is just a small window on some of the dangerous situations I thoughtlessly slid into. It's a miracle that I didn't end up on the nightly news.

Once I was an innocent little boy—*Stevie* my mom called me. At the ages of four, five, and six, seeing swallowtail butterflies flutter around our home in the Hollywood Hills filled me with wonder. I still remember the first time I spied a grasshopper in a vacant lot around the corner from our house. *What a neat looking creature!* I thought delightedly. The bulging eyes and jointed feet totally fascinated me. Such innocent pleasure! Years later, the wonder was gone. Now my own eyes bulged with bloodshot dullness, my breath stank with the smell of liquor, and my legs wobbled at 3 A.M. More than once, I collapsed with an aching stomach in front of a toilet as I vomited up the contents of my "pleasures."

During that eventful summer of '79, at the very time that I was carrying a black Bible by day to my assignments as an extra, I was visiting by night some of Hollywood's darkest streets and indulging in activities that almost ruined my life. In 1981, AIDS hit Los Angeles. It could have been me. One night, after another round of dangerous foolishness, I remember driving alone on a dirty little street just above Hollywood Boulevard. When I reached a stop sign, an icy impression entered my head. I thought about Bible verses I had recently read that spoke about God and the day of judgment. *If there is a God, I'm in trouble, big trouble,* I thought. I pressed the brakes, slowed the car, and turned the corner. Suddenly, I knew I needed to slow my *life* and turn a corner. If I didn't change, I was ruined. But could I? Did I really want to? Not really. So, a war raged within me.

During the closing weeks of that summer, I continued working as an extra around Studio City and Hollywood. Sometimes I took the Bible with me on assignments; sometimes I didn't. *Job. Song of Solomon. Jeremiah. Daniel. Hosea. Amos.* I kept browsing through the smaller books inside the bigger Book. Most verses I hardly understood, but the meaning of others was too plain to miss. Mark Twain said something to the effect that while some people were bothered by what they couldn't understand in the Bible, he was bothered by the things he could understand and *didn't want to do.* That fit me perfectly.

One day I remembered that the man at the beach suggested that if I wanted to learn about the end of the world, I should read some prophecy books. So I checked for Christian bookstores in the Yellow Pages and discovered there was one on Lankershim Boulevard in Studio City, not far from our home. I drove the short distance, walked inside, found the Prophecy section, scanned the shelves, and noticed a book called *The Late, Great Planet Earth* by Hal Lindsey. It looked interesting. On the same shelf were two other books by the same author: *Satan Is Alive and Well on Planet Earth* and *The Terminal Generation.* I bought them all. Now my spiritual library included four books, three by Hal Lindsey and a black Bible. In a short time, I read every Lindsey book.

During those days, I had a close friend named David, a handsome African-American young man. We often went to discos together to dance and meet girls. Unknown to me, Dave was raised a Jehovah's Witness, although he surely wasn't practicing his faith around me. One afternoon as we sat in my bedroom smoking dope and listening to rock groups like Blue Oyster Cult, Electric Light Orchestra, David Bowie, Steely Dan, and Uriah Heep, somehow our conversation turned to religion. "I've been reading the Bible," I muttered.

"No! You're joking!" Dave replied in shocked disbelief. Then he said, "Well, if you're going to get into religion, the least I can do is point you in the right direction. You should meet my grandmother. She's a Jehovah's Witness and will explain everything."

Why not? I asked myself. *This should be interesting.* So, within a week or so, I drove to the apartment of Dave's grandmother for a visit. I saw her only that one time and remember hardly anything she said. But I do recall a stack of books sitting on her table and that she handed me two of them; one blue, the other red. *The Truth That Leads to Eternal Life* and *Thy Kingdom Come* were the titles. "Thanks," I said awkwardly. Now I had six books in my library, three by Hal Lindsey, two by Jehovah's Witnesses, and one black Bible.

I read the Jehovah's Witnesses books also. Mostly, as with Hal Lindsey's works, they didn't make much sense to me. But I do remember that they contained a number of Bible passages that cut me deep—verses such as: "Now the works of the flesh are evident, which are: adultery, fornication, uncleanness, lewdness, idolatry, sorcery, hatred, contentions, jealousies, outbursts of wrath, selfish ambitions, dissensions, heresies, envy, murders, drunkenness, revelries, and the like; of which I tell you before-hand, just as I also told you in time past, that those who practice such things will not inherit the kingdom of God" (Galatians 5:19–21). And, " 'The cowardly, unbelieving, abominable, mur-derers, sexually immoral, sorcerers, idolaters, and all liars shall have their part in the lake which burns with fire and brimstone, which is the second death' " (Revelation 21:8).

Double ouch! Words like "selfish ambitions," "drunkenness," "revelries," "sexually immoral," and "all liars," struck me hard. They were like spiked fists swinging out from the pages and clob-bering me in the face. I had never read anything like this before.

Looking back, I think the main thing I absorbed from Mr. Lindsey's books concerned the devil—that he exists, was kicked out of heaven, and is a seducer. What I remember from those two Jehovah's Witness books is the Bible verses warning that those who live in sin would share the devil's fate by ending up in a hor-rible place called " 'the lake that burns with fire' " (Revelation 21:8, RSV). Satan, sin, and certain punishment awaited sin-ners—these were new, terrifying ideas.

I started feeling like a passenger on a Carnival cruise who sud-denly realized that the ship was about to sail off the edge of the world, or like someone aboard the *Titanic* who had discovered that the "unsinkable ship" was doomed to hit the ice and go down. Yet my fellow passengers had no idea. "Pass the beer!" everyone seemed to be saying as the women grew looser, the dancing sexier, and the music louder. But Bible verses were opening my eyes word by word, line by line, text by text. If this was all true, I didn't like the idea of burning in some lake of fire. No indeed!

Here's another twist: At the same time I began reading the Bible, my father began exploring the mystical world of metaphysics and reading the works of notable New Age authors like Alice Bailey and Benjamin Crème. In his quest, he even visited a spirit medium, who, upon entering a trancelike state, became the unconscious conduit for an invisible entity who identified himself as "Jock." This ghostly personage, who spoke with a distinct accent, claimed to be the disembodied spirit of an eighteenth-century Irishman. Speaking authoritatively from "the other side," Jock claimed an ability to peer into my dad's future. He also offered spiritual guidance—for a fee, of course. Interestingly enough, Jock never mentioned the Bible.

One time my father invited one of his New Age friends to our home for supper. During a candlelit dinner, my dad, Anne, and I sat in rapt attention as our guest explained the secrets of the universe. "Earth's outer atmosphere is filled with souls circling our planet," this metaphysical expert informed us. "These souls are awaiting opportunities to enter new bodies to continue their karmic journey on earth."

Wow, that's different, I thought. *Could it be true?* I looked long and hard at my father. Even though my dad wasn't a disco dancer, he had always been my best friend. I loved him so much. I distinctly remember carrying on a little debate within myself. It went something like this: *Hmm . . . My dad believes this guy, yet his ideas are totally different from what the black Book says. Are they right or wrong? On the one hand, if they're wrong and the Bible is right, then I need to make some major changes in my life to avoid that lake of fire. But what if my dad and our guest are right? That would mean I'd be giving up lots of fun for nothing. There are no fiery consequences to worry about if I mess up; my soul will simply return to earth in someone else's body. That doesn't sound too bad. What should I do? What should I believe? What is the truth? I'm not sure. But I do know this—I like smoking dope, and I don't really want to change.*

As this conversation rattled within my brain, I glanced again at my dad. Then I thought about the Bible. Dad, Bible, Dad, Bible, Dad, Bible . . . Which one? Aghh! That night I concluded, *Enough! There's no one like my dad! I love and trust him more than anyone else. He's never let me down. He's always been there for me. Wherever he goes, I'll go. Bye bye, Bible.*

That night I made a definite choice to follow my father. After all, he had taken wonderful care of me for twenty years, so why shouldn't I follow him? Since I'd started reading the Bible, I had also begun feeling something I hadn't struggled with before: a sense of guilt. This was new to me—and unpleasant. Let me clarify: When I had done bad things before, like snorting cocaine or stealing, I knew they were wrong, but I thought the only thing to worry about was getting caught. Those acts didn't bother my conscience very much. But as I read the Book, a new moral sense unexpectedly rose up within me, and the notion of accountability—even a day of judgment—invaded my complacent world like the flashing red lights on a police car. Yet after that meal with our metaphysical guest, my mind was relieved. Reading the Bible was all just a phase, but now it was over—finished. *Hello, Hollywood!*

Then I met Paula at a disco somewhere in the San Fernando Valley. She was younger than me—probably seventeen, while I was twenty. We hit it off right away. We swayed on dance floors under strobe lights, snuggled together at drive-in theaters, guzzled alcohol, and became quite "physical" at my house when my dad and Anne weren't home, which was something all my friends did. Purity, self-control, and "waiting until marriage" were things we knew nothing about. Paula was quiet, attractive, and unrestricted when we were alone. Every time we went on a date, we crossed moral lines. I'll leave it at that.

Oddly enough (not really, but it was unexpected), my conscience started pestering me again. *What's up with this? I'm finished with the Bible, so why is this happening to me?* Double aghh! I didn't realize it at the time, but it's now clear to me that a heavenly Lover with higher standards than Paula or me was in hot pursuit of my soul. He doesn't give up easily. I knew little about Him and had just purposely rejected Him. "Go away!" I'd said. "Can't You see that I'm not interested?" This was my clear message to the Author of the black Book. But He was deaf to my stubbornness.

My internal struggle intensified as two invisible supernatural powers wrestled over me. Was it a Monday, Tuesday, or Friday? I don't remember; but at some point I ignored my former decision and grabbed the Book. *Hosea. Joel. Jonah. Zephaniah. Zechariah. . . .* Then a day or two later, I'd say to myself, "Forget it, where's Paula?" And she was waiting. Yet, after another hot date with my seventeen-year-old sweetheart, a not-of-this-world influence would push me back to the Book.

During those back-and-forth days, I often tried to obliterate the voice of my conscience by listening to deafening sounds from some of my favorite rock bands: Deep Purple, Jethro Tull, Tom Petty, and the Eagles. But another note was growing louder inside my head. In reality, I was hearing two conflicting tunes originating from opposite ends of the universe: In one, electric guitars and the drum sets of earth were pounding notes perfectly agreeable to my base human nature and network of friends. The other stood separate from Hollywood's if-it-feels-good-do-it values. It was foreign, alien—a Voice from the Book. Louder . . . louder . . .

louder, like someone beyond the stars turning up a moral volume control knob inside my brain. Try as I might to turn it off, it wouldn't go away. Normal sleep left me.

The Book says, "The flesh lusts against the Spirit, and the Spirit against the flesh; *and these are contrary to one another*" (Galatians 5:17, emphasis added). This verse describes a war zone—not one in Iraq, Afghanistan, Israel, or the West Bank, but within human hearts. The phrase "the flesh" applies to our fallen human nature, which tends toward depravity as effortlessly as water flows downhill. The line "the flesh lusts against the Spirit, and the Spirit against the flesh" reveals the intense conflict between the Holy Spirit—a moral force that pulls upward—and our own self-destructive tendencies that seek to drag us down. Caught in the crossfire, I felt like I was being ripped apart. You've heard the question "Are we having fun yet?" I wasn't.

At the time, I found it impossible to step back objectively, see the big picture, and realize that my own natural tendencies were slowly destroying me. Because I was still smoking dope and drinking heavily, things were blurry. Jimmy Hendrix's heavy-metal song "Purple Haze" fit me perfectly. Poor Jimmy. He was a 1960s rock legend who overdosed on drugs and suffocated in his own vomit, joining Janis Joplin, Sid Vicious, Jimmy Morrison, Elvis Presley, and Andy Gibb as another Hollywood star whose light was snuffed out in darkness. I wasn't that far gone, but I knew something was wrong. It was becoming as plain as the fact that a rabbi is Jewish. I was unhappy, empty, and scared. A gaping hole had been ripped into my heart. Nevertheless, at that moment, approximately 65 percent of me wasn't interested in changing.

Not yet.

6

My Search Begins

"As long as one keeps searching, the answers come."
~ Joan Baez (1941–),
American folksinger

While still desiring Hollywood's tantalizing nightlife, a growing part of me felt a longing for new friends—friends of a different kind. My regular party pals weren't really "bad guys"—I mean, they didn't beat up people or hurt old ladies. They were just wild and crazy, like me. Rock concerts, parties, beer, and women—that's what we lived for. Yet Michael, the young man who'd invited me to church, was different. He was about my age, a strong Christian, studying for the ministry. I realized I needed to meet more people like him. But where? The Baptist church in downtown Los Angeles was simply too far from Studio City.

First stop: the synagogue. Right down the street from my father's condo in Studio City was the synagogue where my brother Mike received his bar mitzvah. *I may not be a good Jew, but I'm still Jewish,* I thought, *so why not check it out?* Driving two minutes from our home to a synagogue located near the intersection of Colfax and Moorpark, I parked my car and knocked on the door. The rabbi wasn't there. Actually, no one was there. *So much for Judaism,* I mused and drove away. (To this day, my mother wishes the rabbi had been there and that I had found God through Judaism. Sorry, Mom, but that's not what happened!)

Next idea: find a church. But which one? I knew hardly any Christians. In fact, I had no intelligent concept of what a Christian, Buddhist, Hindu, Moslem, or even a Jew really was. As I sat in my downstairs bedroom contemplating my next step, I remembered that I had found a Christian bookstore in the Yellow Pages. *Maybe I can find a church there also,* I thought. Turning the pages, I checked under "churches" and found more than I expected. *Wow! There sure are a lot of churches in the world!*

Scanning the listings in the Studio City/North Hollywood area, I randomly pinpointed a Methodist church located nearby. Hopping into my car again, I took a short trip, and this time, the pastor was there. I don't remember his name, but he was very friendly. Taking me into his office, he asked how he might be of service.

"I'm Steve Wohlberg, from Studio City, and I guess you could say I'm checking out churches. What do you think about hell?" I asked point-blank.

I need to press the Rewind button and explain why I asked that particular question. On my first or second visit to the Baptist church on Slausen Avenue, Pastor Harper and his wife invited me to their home for a friendly chat. They were very nice people.

"Are you willing to pray the sinner's prayer?" Pastor Harper inquired as we stood in his living room.

"Err . . . ah . . . I guess so," I stuttered, having no idea what this meant.

The pastor grasped my hands and told me to repeat what he said. So, I dutifully mouthed some short phrases about God taking over my life. I'm sure Pastor Harper's intentions were good, but I didn't understand much of what he said—although, in retrospect, I think this was the very first prayer my lips ever uttered (maybe God wrote it down in my heavenly baby book). So, I was making progress, and it felt good.

Then something significant happened. We sat down, and with his finger, Pastor Harper drew an imaginary circle on his living-room table. "Steve," he said earnestly, "imagine that this circle is our universe. At the end of the world, God will take those who aren't saved and will send them to a place called 'outer darkness' or 'hell' (he pointed outside the circle), where they will be tormented throughout all eternity. We may not like the idea, but that's what the Bible says."

My eyes widened, and I stared at him, speechless. I vaguely remembered reading something about "the lake of fire" in one of the books I had read earlier, but this was the first time someone had sat me down and explained it like this. The concept terrified me. That is all I remember about our conversation that day—the sinner's prayer and hell.

As I headed home that Sunday afternoon, I noticed the numerous billboards that lined the freeway. Many of them pictured smiling people doing common, everyday things. *They're going to hell,* I thought. *So are most people: my dad, my mom, my brother, my sister—all of them. They'll be plunged into outer darkness at the end of the world and be tormented forever!* It all seemed so surreal.

That night as my dad and Anne slept peacefully in their upstairs bedroom, I slowly walked up the two flights of stairs and then collapsed right outside their closed door, weeping uncontrollably. Now, I wasn't an emotional kid; I didn't even cry when my parents divorced. But for some reason, Pastor Harper's words about hell hit me hard. I love my dad. As I've said already, throughout my wild teenage years we remained close, like best friends. He had never read the Bible in his entire life, and as far as I knew, he believed that after death his karmic soul would circle earth until it found another body to inhabit. I couldn't bear the thought of him sizzling forever in some fiery black hole.

Then the bedroom door opened and my dad stepped out. "Steve!" He asked in shock, "What on earth are you crying about?"

"Dad, I know you don't believe this, but I learned today from Pastor Harper that if you don't believe in Jesus Christ, you'll spend eternity suffering in hell!"

Dad just stared at me, eyes big, speechless.

I was so distraught that a few days later, Dad and Anne sent me to a psychologist. I think they found him in the Yellow Pages. His office was on Ventura Boulevard in Studio City, just minutes from our home. I drove over, parked my car, walked upstairs, was ushered into his plush office, and sat down.

"What seems to be the problem?" the psychologist inquired with a look of genuine concern. "Your parents sent you here; what's wrong?"

"Well, I recently started reading the Bible and going to church, and I just learned that if my relatives don't believe in Jesus, they're going to hell. This scares me. I'm all worked up about it. That's it."

The psychologist sat back quietly, took a deep breath, and then said something like, "Steve, what you learned is true. I'm a Christian too. So is my whole family. We all believe in hell. That's what the Bible says."

It was a short conversation. I drove home.

Fast-forward to the Methodist minister again: "What do you believe about hell?" I asked him. "This subject really bothers me."

He leaned back in his chair and stared at me. *Hmm*, he may have thought, *twenty years old. Jewish. Just starting to read the Bible. Disturbed about hell.* After sitting thoughtfully for a moment, he reached for a small electrical fan whizzing on his desk. "Look at this fan," he said. "See how it's connected to the wall by this power cord? This illustrates our relationship to God. The Lord created us all, gives us life, and keeps us running whether we believe in Him or not. If people choose their sins instead of Him, at the end of the world He will do the best thing a merciful God can do"—and with that, he jerked the plug out of the wall.

Fascinated, I watched as the whizzing fan decelerated . . . slower . . . slower . . . slower . . . until it stopped completely.

"This is what will happen to those who are lost," the minister commented. "Without God's power to keep them running, they'll stop, just like this fan."

His illustration seemed to make sense, but now I was confused. Who was right—Pastor Harper or this minister? The minister prayed for me and told me I was welcome in his church anytime, and then I left. I don't know why, but I never visited his church.

That eventful summer ended, and I put my assignments as an extra on hold. It was finally time for me to move out of my father's house and live on my own. This would be a big step for me, but a boy has to become a man sometime, right?

After brief consideration, my family decided that I should enroll at California State University of Northridge (CSUN) in the San Fernando Valley, not far from Studio City. Packing my bags, I vacated my psychedelic bedroom and moved into a dormitory near CSUN for my third year of college. *I don't think I'll ever make a living as an extra,* I thought. *My dad is a businessman. He makes good money. I might as well follow in his steps.*

Arriving at the dorm, I quickly discovered I had a roommate; I don't remember his name. Marijuana breezes floated down the hallway. *Smells familiar,* I thought to myself. Our dorm was officially co-ed, which means there were girls living just a few doors away. Every Saturday night, the dormitory cafeteria was transformed into a discothèque, strobe lights and all. CSUN school life was permeated with the same scene I knew so well. So Hollywoodish.

Now, however, I was struggling with whether to participate or not. Part of me wanted to meet those girls, smoke that pot, and bounce around on that cafeteria floor. Another part of me screamed, "Don't do it!" Only a few weeks earlier, Pastor Harper had led me in the sinner's prayer. If I chose the ladies and dance floor, would I burn forever? Or would my fan simply stop running, like the Methodist pastor said? I didn't know. But I knew one thing: Neither option sounded pleasant. Regardless of the final fate of souls, my spiritual life had been awakened, and even if it was only for selfish reasons, I *did* want to keep living. Definitely. My desire for change had grown from about 65 percent to about 85 percent. More progress.

I chose marketing as my major and a minor in public relations. On registration day, I drove to the university and lined up with other students in the administration building to enroll in my classes. I didn't know a soul. When I was growing up in Studio City and North Hollywood, many of my childhood friends had transitioned with me from Carpenter Avenue Elementary School to Walter Reed Jr. High and then to North Hollywood High. A handful had moved on with me for a two-year term at Los Angeles Valley College. But I was the only one of that group at CSUN. I was a small fish in a big pond of strangers. Not only that, but I was now searching into religion, which I assumed wouldn't be a popular topic among pot smokers.

Wandering around outside the administration building, I noticed a row of booths manned by students promoting various activities, clubs, fraternities, and sororities. Passing from booth to booth, I reached a table that, to my great surprise, was manned by Christians from Calvary Chapel. A couple of people sat there handing out literature and talking to passing students. I stopped, was quickly noticed, and had a short visit with one of the guys. Placing some flyers in my hand, a young man cordially invited me to attend an off-campus Bible study and to meet other believers.

This is different. I thought. *There was nothing like this at North Hollywood High.* "Thanks, I'll check it out," I told him, and walked away.

A couple days later, I walked into a large building somewhere near CSUN and entered a room filled with young people who were singing songs I had never heard before. The atmosphere was quite different from the raunchy parties and smoke-filled concert halls I was so familiar with. There was no alcohol, and the music wasn't about sex, drugs, and rock 'n' roll, but about heaven, God's love, and the gift of salvation through a Man who died on a cross. There was a mixture of guys and gals, all college-age, many of them holding Bibles. Everyone was smiling and friendly to each other and to me.

Then something happened that puzzled me. One of the group leaders who was playing a guitar began talking about the return of Jesus and how we would all be "raptured" to heaven in "the twinkling of an eye." I knew nothing about this. "Let's practice!" he said. "On the count of three, I want everyone to jump as high as you can and shout *'rapture!'* Ready? One, two, three . . . *'Rapture!'* "

We all leaped into the air and yelled a couple of times. It seemed a bit silly, but it was fun. And it was more wholesome than being surrounded by scantily clad women while gyrating with bloodshot eyes on some dance floor.

After the Bible study, I returned to the dorm and slept—living away from home for the first time in my life; at a new school; enrolled in my third year of college; with a new schedule of classes about to begin; and a stack of textbooks covering economics, statistics, and public relations. Still Jewish, I had either met or been influenced by graffiti sprayed on a rock, a man with a loudspeaker in the back of a pickup, a young girl on Hollywood Boulevard, a man with a tattered Bible near UCLA, a dark-haired gal who believed she had seen demons at a party, an extra who warned about the approaching end of the age, three books by Hal Lindsey, a black Baptist church in downtown LA, Pastor Harper, an elderly Jehovah's Witness woman who was the grandmother of one of my disco buddies, a psychologist on Ventura Boulevard, a Methodist minister, and a group from Calvary Chapel doing rapture drills.

What would happen next?

7

It Is
Written

*"Give me good digestion, Lord,
and something worth digesting."*
~ Author unknown

I miss my old home, I thought after a week or two of dormitory living. Cal State Northridge was only about thirty minutes from Studio City via Northridge streets and Interstate 101. So, one weekend I took the short trip and slept in my old room. Dad and Anne were glad to see me. It was nice to be home.

That Sunday morning I woke up and at some point decided to watch TV in the upstairs den, the same room where I'd found my stepmother's black Bible. Was I looking for anything special that day? I don't think so.

Casually poking the On button on the remote control, I began channel surfing. Within a few minutes, a program caught my eye. "Hello, friend," said a distinguished, pleasant-looking man in his early sixties. He was George Vandeman, host of the international TV show *It Is Written,* sponsored by the Seventh-day Adventist Church. Pastor Vandeman's topic that morning was the Bible Sabbath. Although I was Jewish, I knew nothing at all about the

Sabbath. Our family didn't observe holy days, eat a kosher diet, or do practically anything that religious Jews do.

Pastor Vandeman's manner of speaking appealed to me. Holding the Bible in his hands, that day he read passages about the Ten Commandments and then specifically about the fourth commandment, which states, " 'The seventh day is the Sabbath of the LORD' " (Exodus 20:10). Pastor Vandeman then said that even though millions of wonderful, God-fearing Christians go to church every Sunday, "the seventh day" was really Saturday, not Sunday. This intrigued me.

At the end of his half-hour program, Pastor Vandeman held up a small book titled *A Day to Remember*. Smiling warmly through the TV set and apparently looking right at me, he said, "Friend, if you want to read this book, just call the toll-free number on the screen, and we'll mail it to you for free." Looking back, I remember sensing some sort of spiritual urge nudging me to get off the couch, walk over to the phone, and make the call. *Why not?* I thought. *I've visited with Baptists, Methodists, Jehovah's Witnesses, and a collegiate group from Calvary Chapel. Why not check out this Sabbath thing?* So, I made the call.

A few days later, the book showed up in my dad's mailbox. Upon receiving it, I sat down on the living-room couch and read it in one sitting. As with Hal Lindsey's books and my perusal of the Bible so far, I didn't understand everything I read. But I remember vividly realizing that when the Ten Commandments were first given, they had been inscribed not on manmade paper by any human being but on "two tables of the testimony, tables of stone, *written with the finger of God*" (Exodus 31:18, RSV, emphasis added).

Wow, I thought, *that's impressive!* I stopped reading, set the book on my lap, and stared off into space in intense contemplation. What happened next wasn't a vision or prophetic revelation, but at that moment, I beheld a crystal-clear mental image of the

Ten Commandments rising high in the sky. *God's law written on stone,* I thought. *This is powerful stuff!*

Soon, an internal dialogue began: *Am I ever confused about religion! Everywhere I go, someone says something different. How can I know what's right?* Then this thought hit me forcibly: *If I stick to the Ten Commandments, I can't go wrong.* This appeared unquestionably reasonable.

Still staring off into space, I started mentally reviewing the Ten Commandments one by one:

1. You shall have no other gods before Me.
2. You shall not make any graven images. . . .
3. You shall not take the Name of the Lord your God in vain. . . .
4. Remember the Sabbath day to keep it holy. . . . The seventh day is the Sabbath of the Lord your God. . . .
5. Honor your father and mother. . . .
6. You shall not kill.
7. You shall not commit adultery.
8. You shall not steal.
9. You shall not bear false witness. . . .
10. You shall not covet. . . . (See Exodus 20:3–17.)

"Remember the Sabbath day. . . . *The seventh day* is the Sabbath of the Lord." I suddenly remembered Hal Lindsey's book, *Satan Is Alive and Well on Planet Earth.* Then another thought struck me: *If there is a real devil, is it possible that he has worked behind the scenes to lead most Christians to go to church on the wrong day?* As usual, I wasn't sure, but my interest was piqued. I wanted to find out. Picking up the book, I finished it in short order.

At the end of *A Day to Remember,* I noticed a sentence that said something like, "If you would like to learn more about the

Bible Sabbath, visit a Seventh-day Adventist church." Then I realized that the *It Is Written* TV program and *A Day to Remember* were connected to a group called Seventh-day Adventists. That name was entirely new to me, just as the names Baptist, Methodist, Jehovah's Witnesses, and Calvary Chapel had been. Or was it? A tiny, hazy memory floated up. *Wait a minute. Haven't I heard that name before? I think so . . . somewhere. Where?* Moments later, an answer flashed into my brain: *At a health-food store in Northridge. Yes, a man who belongs to the Seventh-day Adventist Church works at a health-food store in Northridge!*

Rewind again: Three or four months earlier, I was buying food at a Northridge health-food store with Steve, one of my closest friends—the same friend who talked to that young man in Westwood. (Believe it or not, even though Steve and I both smoked dope heavily and craved cocaine, we were also health-food lovers who frequented natural markets to purchase avocado-sprout sandwiches on wholegrain bread, healthy salads, and fruit smoothies!) That particular day, while I was filling a cart with tofu burgers, almond butter, soy ice cream, sesame sticks, and other natural goodies, Steve had struck up a conversation with an employee who was spraying water on vegetables in the produce section.

"Did you see that guy I was talking to?" Steve asked me as we strolled out of the market. "He's a Seventh-day Adventist."

So? I thought indifferently. It meant nothing to me at the time. I didn't know anyone from that church. In fact, that was the first time I had ever heard that name. I had no reason to remember it either; yet somehow it lodged inside one or two brain cells.

Having read the invitation in the back of *A Day to Remember*, I was determined to find that Seventh-day Adventist. So, a day or two later, I hopped into my car and drove to the health-food store in Northridge, searching for the mystery man who'd sprayed the vegetables. I parked my car, entered the store, looked around, and, lo and behold, there he was, standing by the smoothie bar! Without a moment's hesitation, I walked straight over to him, reached out my hand in greeting, and said, "Hi, my name is Steve Wohlberg. Would you mind if I went to church with you on Saturday?" He was probably a bit stunned, for people rarely approach Adventists and ask to be taken to church. However, the man's answer wasn't long in coming. "Sure," he said. "I'm Richard."

"What do you believe about hell?" I blurted out almost immediately, not being one to beat around the bush.

What happened next appeared highly significant to me. Without knowing anything about my visit with Pastor Harper, Richard raised his finger and drew a circle in the air. "Imagine this is the universe," the tall, blondish-haired man said earnestly. "A long time ago, the entire universe was clean. God created angels, and they all lived happily together, until one of God's top angels, whose name was Lucifer, turned against his Creator and committed what the Bible calls 'sin.' "

I listened intently.

Richard continued, "Other angels followed Lucifer, and so did Adam and Eve. This was like placing a cancerous blot inside God's pure universe." Richard placed a finger in the center of his imaginary circle to illustrate how sin upset things. I got the picture.

"When sin has run its course, God will erase this dark blot that has caused so much pain. Then once again His entire universe will be happy, clean, and filled with love forever." Richard rotated his hand as if he were wielding an eraser and then waited for my response.

Although I determined to study this hell topic more fully in the days ahead, at that moment something inside me went "click." Richard's words made sense. It seemed reasonable and sensible to me that a loving God could—and eventually would—entirely eradicate the devil, sin, and all evil so that His universe would be filled with only good things again. Richard had made a favorable first impression.

My response was, "When can we go to church?"

"The next Saturday you're free," Richard enthusiastically replied.

Time to check out the Adventists, I mused.

Soon, Richard took me to his church in Canoga Park, not far from Northridge. The people there were friendly, like the members of Pastor Harper's church in downtown LA. Richard introduced me to his pastor, whose last name, interestingly enough, was Church.

"How did you find out about us?" Pastor Church inquired after the church service.

"By watching George Vandeman, reading a book, and finding Richard in a health-food store," I replied.

Surveying my young face with pleasant interest, Pastor Church quickly said, "Let's visit in my office."

Sitting in the pastor's office, I noticed shelves of books lining the walls. By this time, I owned three books by Mr. Lindsey, two from Jehovah's Witnesses, some literature from Calvary Chapel, and one black Bible, and I still wanted to expand my library. After some brief "let's get acquainted" conversation, Pastor Church noticed my eyes scanning the books behind his desk. "Do you like to read?" he inquired.

"Well, I did when I was a kid," I said, "but I quit in my teen years. Now I'm starting again."

Then, eyeing a book on his shelf, I asked eagerly, "What's that one about?"

Sensing that I wasn't ready for heavy theology, the pastor bypassed my choice and grabbed a medium-size hardcover volume bearing the intriguing title *The Desire of Ages.* This book was written by a remarkable nineteenth-century woman named Ellen G. White, who developed the reputation of being led by God as she wrote. But of this I had no knowledge.

"Try this one," Pastor Church recommended, holding out *The Desire of Ages*. "It's about the life of Jesus Christ. You can have it."

"Thanks, Pastor! Thank you very much."

After Pastor Church kindly offered a prayer for me, I returned to my dorm. I didn't realize it, but that book was destined to become a channel for influences that would change my life forever. I sincerely hope you'll read the following pages with an open heart. You'll be amazed at what you find.

8

Hooked by a Book

*"A good book retains its interior heat
and will warm a generation yet unborn."*
~ Clifton Fadiman (1904–1999),
American writer, radio-show host

Back inside my dorm room, I surveyed with increasing disinterest my stack of textbooks, especially statistics and economics. *What have I gotten myself into?* I thought. Throughout my teenage years, like a frog out of water, I had hopped from job to job without any clear sense of purpose or direction. Sports, trout fishing, sporadic employment, rock music, TV, movies, lazy days, crazy nights—that's all I knew. I chose marketing as my CSUN major, not from deep motivation or careful thought but because my dad was a businessman and I figured it was time for me to settle into something stable and to start making some real money, especially since I was living on my own for the first time in my life. The chances of any future escalation from Hollywood extra to wealthy stardom seemed pie-in-the-sky. So I chose a business career.

My dorm room was small, like most dorm rooms: four walls, two beds, two desks, and one door into a shared bathroom.

Theoretically, dormitory rooms are supposed to be places where thoughtful students energetically study textbooks, gain useful knowledge, and take practical steps toward accomplishing something in life. Realistically, they're often party holes—places where set-free-from-parents guys and gals mess around, drink liquor, smoke dope, and someone gets pregnant. Late one night, I opened my dorm door to discover men and women on both beds. I didn't join my roommate or his friends in their activities that evening.

But the smoke disappeared, the air cleared, and I soon found myself alone again in a tiny room at the start of my third year of college—thirty minutes from my father's house and about half as far from my mother, brother, and sister, who had relocated into an apartment in Encino. Statistics, economics, Baptists, Methodists, Jehovah's Witnesses, Calvary Chapel, rapture drills, *It Is Written,* Adventists, hell, Saturday, Sunday, God, Satan? *Oi vey!*—what was right? What was I going to do with my life? The sights, sounds, and smells of wild living still surrounded me, seeping under my door and into my head. I felt lonely, directionless, and confused.

There it sat. *The Desire of Ages.* Book seven in my spiritual library. Textbooks demanded my attention, but this volume beckoned voicelessly, "Pick me up. Read me." I don't remember what day it was—Monday, Tuesday, or Wednesday—but at some point, a twenty-year-old Jewish college student named Steve Wohlberg enrolled in marketing at Cal State University of Northridge picked up that book and began reading the story of a Man named Jesus Christ.

I had read Ecclesiastes and Proverbs, meandered through Psalms, and read isolated sections of other books in both the Old and New Testaments. But mostly, the Bible was like Greek to me. I grasped only small portions of the passages—perhaps 15 percent. As I've said, I didn't grow up reading the Bible, and this whole religion thing was about as natural to me as an octopus in Yosemite. The message of the Bible grew slowly in my mind. Even though my conscience had been awakened enough to motivate me to visit different churches, I was still heavily under the influence of my upbringing and environment. Hollywood remained in me. I still smoked dope.

The first chapter of *The Desire of Ages* started with the big picture, taking me back even before the creation of planet Earth to a time when a magnificent Maker decided to create a group of highly intelligent entities called *angels,* the brightest and most powerful of whom was an exalted personality named Lucifer, "son of the morning" (Isaiah 14:12). Explaining the subtle process that turned Lucifer into the devil, *The Desire of Ages* reported: "Sin originated in self-seeking. Lucifer, the covering cherub, desired to be first in heaven. He sought to gain control of heavenly beings, to draw them away from their Creator, and to win their homage to himself. Therefore he misrepresented God, attributing to Him the desire for self-exaltation. With his own evil characteristics he sought to invest the loving Creator. Thus he deceived angels. Thus he deceived men."[1]

I had never really thought about the invisible world until that dark-haired woman at Denny's restaurant blurted out at 4 A.M., "Steve, I think I saw the devil!" A month or so later, Hal Lindsey's *Satan Is Alive and Well on Planet Earth* supplied biblical information, stressing the reality of demonic forces. Now *The Desire of Ages* repeated those same truths and added the insight that Lucifer's rebellion was rooted in his own "self-seeking" and his subsequent *modus operandi* has been to attribute his own aberrant evil to God's loving heart, creating distrust of God's goodness. That's how he deceived angels above and men below. Thus, through reading *The Desire of Ages* in my dorm room, I learned that the core issue in the cosmic conflict now raging between the Creator and His former chief officer concerns *what kind of person God is.*

Does He really love His creatures? Is He just, fair, and worth serving?

Shifting from Lucifer's rebellion in heaven to the spiritual struggle now being waged on earth, *The Desire of Ages* continued: "The earth was dark through misapprehension of God. That the gloomy shadows might be lightened, that the world might be brought back to God, Satan's deceptive power was to be broken. This could not be done by force. The exercise of force is contrary to the principles of God's government; He desires only the service of love; and love cannot be commanded; it cannot be won by force or authority. Only by love is love awakened. To know God is to love Him; His character must be manifested in contrast to the character of Satan. This work only one Being in all the universe could do. Only He who knew the height and depth of the love of God could make it known. Upon the world's dark night the Sun of Righteousness must rise, 'with healing in His wings.' "[2]

I don't know whether these words speak to your heart, but they hooked me. They told me what I needed to hear. They said that life's greatest accomplishment isn't achieving a college education, earning a degree, or landing a high-paying job, as important as these are. It is in having "gloomy shadows" lifted from our sin-darkened minds so we can discern "the height and depth of the love of God." What I needed most was a clear picture of my Maker. *The Desire of Ages* declared that only one Person in the entire universe could reveal that picture without marring it. A Jewish prophet named Malachi called that Person "the Sun of Righteousness" and said He would "rise, 'with healing in His wings' " (see Malachi 4:2).

Chapter two of *The Desire of Ages*, "The Chosen People," was about the ancient Jewish nation. Of course, this interested me because, well, I'm Jewish. I read that God loved Israel, chose Israel, called Israel, and committed to Israel special truths about the coming Messiah—truths taught by prophets. Yet *The Desire of Ages* declared that soon after the chosen nation entered the Promised Land, a large portion of its religion lost its vitality and degenerated into formalism.

My own upbringing seemed to fall into this category. A few Passovers with neighbors, an empty chair for Elijah (Eli*who?*), lighting candles during Hanukkah (I hardly knew what the term meant), watching Mike's bar mitzvah—to me, this was religion. Messages from prophets? Promises and plans of the living God? Not only was I woefully ignorant of these things, but I discovered that a large percentage of ancient Israel was in the same boat. When the greatest event in history finally hit—the arrival of the Predicted One—many of God's own people were caught off guard.

The next chapter, " 'The Fullness of the Time,' " described the condition of the mighty Roman Empire two thousand years ago. Her vast territories were filled with magnificent temples, heathen statues, and sun-worshiping prostitutes who enticed pleasure lovers. While philosophers split hairs over the exact nature of the soul and its relationship to physical matter, the morals of men and women steadily spiraled downward into gross sensuality, vice, and corruption. In a nutshell, the world back then was a mess.

"The fullness of the time had come. Humanity, becoming more degraded through ages of transgression, called for the coming of the Redeemer. Satan had been working to make the gulf deep and impassable between earth and heaven. By his falsehoods he had emboldened men in sin. It was his purpose to wear out the forbearance of God, and to extinguish His love for man, so that He would abandon the world to satanic jurisdiction."[3]

The Roman world seemed a lot like my world in A.D. 1979— teeming with corruption. For years, the smoky atmosphere inside Hollywood nightclubs and parties hadn't bothered me a bit. In fact, I loved it. I craved sensuality and the beat. But now something was happening to me. I was getting tired of strobe lights, cheap thrills, hangovers, and headaches. I was searching for something different.

The Roman world had been equally dark. *The Desire of Ages* informed me that behind this degradation was the cunning activity of an invisible devil whose goal was to "wear out the forbearance of God, and to extinguish His love for man, so that He would abandon the world to satanic jurisdiction." This was Lucifer's master plan.

Two thousand years ago, all heaven wondered how the Holy One would react. Loyal angels sat on the edge of their seats. By this time, I was quite interested myself to discover the answer.

Chapter four, "Unto You a Saviour," revealed what God did. Instead of forsaking us, He sent into earth's dense darkness His most precious gift: His promised Messiah. It said that approximately seven hundred years before this event occurred, a Jewish prophet named Micah even pinpointed the location of His birth: " 'But you, Bethlehem Ephrathah, though you are little among the thousands of Judah, yet out of you shall come forth to Me the One to be Ruler in Israel, whose goings forth are from of old, from everlasting' " (Micah 5:2).

Bethlehem, a tiny town in Judah, would become the birthplace of the Promised One, who was destined to be "Ruler in Israel." Yet He wouldn't originate there. His "goings forth are from of old, from everlasting." Thus, Israel's Messiah has existed from eternity. *That's what Micah said.* There was no mistaking it.

Why hadn't anyone ever told me this? As far as I knew, our rabbi never mentioned it, and my parents had never heard of it. Yet it was there, written plainly in the prophets—along with other prophecies that described the Messiah's lineage, character, and mission.

The saddest thing was that when heaven's clock finally struck the predicted hour of fulfillment, many even within Israel didn't realize what was happening. With deep interest I read, "The Jewish nation had been preserved as a witness that Christ [the Messiah] was to be born of the seed of Abraham and of David's line; yet they knew not that His coming was now at hand. In the temple the morning and the evening sacrifice daily pointed to the Lamb of God; yet even here was no preparation to receive Him. The priests and teachers of that nation knew not that the greatest event of the ages was about to take place.[4]

Slowly, it dawned on me that the title of the book I was reading, *The Desire of Ages*, referred to this very Messiah, the Promised One. *He was the Desire of all ages, who alone could meet the deepest need of every human heart for love.* When He entered history in fulfillment of ancient biblical prophecies, many welcomed Him. Yet others weren't interested. Some accepted Him; others rejected Him. Some saw Him as the answer; others, as a stone of stumbling. Yet according to prophets, He was the " 'Star [to] come out of Jacob' " and the " 'Scepter [to] rise out of Israel' " (Numbers 24:17). He was the Hope of Israel and the world.

One cold night a dazzling light shone above the Bethlehem fields where a shepherd boy named David once guarded his flock. The light came from heavenly messengers whose assignment was to announce to the entire human family that *the Desire of ages had come!*

Now there were in the same country shepherds living out in the fields, keeping watch over their flock by night. And behold, an angel of the Lord stood before them, and the glory of the Lord shone around them, and they were greatly afraid. Then the angel said to them, "Do not be afraid, for behold, I bring you good tidings of great joy which will be to all people. For there is born to you this day in the city of

David a Savior, who is Christ the Lord. And this will *be* the sign to you: You will find a Babe wrapped in swaddling cloths, lying in a manger."

And suddenly there was with the angel a multitude of the heavenly host praising God and saying:

"Glory to God in the highest,
And on earth peace, goodwill toward men!"

So it was, when the angels had gone away from them into heaven, that the shepherds said to one another, "Let us now go to Bethlehem and see this thing that has come to pass, which the Lord has made known to us." And they came with haste and found Mary and Joseph, and the Babe lying in a manger (Luke 2:8–16).

The New Testament says the Messiah "came to His own, and His own did not receive Him. But as many as received Him, to them He gave the right to become children of God" (John 1:11, 12). The chapter "Unto You a Saviour" and subsequent chapters declare that in spite of the unbelief of certain religious leaders, many openhearted people within Israel did discern their Messiah's arrival. Joseph, Mary, Zechariah, Elizabeth, the group of lowly shepherds, Simeon and Anna in the temple—these were all Jews who welcomed His birth.

The Desire of Ages was perfect for me because it explained in a simple way, step by step, event by event, and scene by scene, the story of Jesus Christ. I had never heard any of this before; it was entirely new to me. Set against the larger backdrop of Lucifer's initial heavenly revolt, its unfolding drama gripped my usually short attention span as nothing else had ever done. Sure, I had textbooks to study, and yes, my feet were still on earth at CSUN. But now the story of a Bethlehem Baby whose birth was predicted by prophets and heralded by an angelic choir (that wasn't playing rock music!) captured my interest so ferociously that nothing could stop me from turning pages—*nothing*. I had to know what would happen next.

It is not my intention to summarize every chapter of the book that Pastor Church gave me. Instead, I will focus on its highlights and describe what happened to me. Although the title of this book, *From Hollywood to Heaven,* points to my story, it's a fact that my life changed because of His life. If Jesus' story is new to you, I hope my journey so far has awakened your desire to keep reading. Whether or not you'll believe in Him is up to you.

There's more to come—stick with me!

1. Ellen G. White, *The Desire of Ages* (Nampa, Idaho: Pacific Press®, 1940), 21, 22.
2. Ibid., 22.
3. Ibid., 34, 35.
4. Ibid., 44.

9

"No Man Ever Spoke Like This Man!"

"With the birth of the Babe in Bethlehem, there emerged a great endowment,
a power stronger than weapons, a wealth more lasting than the coins of Caesar."
~ Thomas S. Monson (1927–),
American religious leader and business executive

The world has had its great leaders, teachers, philosophers, scientists, and explorers: Socrates, Plato, Confucius, Galileo, Columbus, Newton, Einstein, Gandhi, Martin Luther King Jr., and countless others. The ideas, philosophies, discoveries, and convictions of these people have affected millions of human beings throughout history and around the world. Yet no teacher, philosopher, politician, theologian, scientist, or guru has influenced more people, fueled more controversy, generated more opposition, inspired more devotion, or transformed more lives than a young Jewish rabbi who boldly declared, " 'I am the light of the world. He who follows Me shall not walk in darkness, but have the light of life' " (John 8:12). Whatever your opinion of Him at this moment, it is significant to realize that more books have been written about Him than about any other person who has ever lived on planet Earth. Ask any librarian. He's bigger than Harry Potter.

After "Jesus was born in Bethlehem of Judea in the days of Herod the king" (Matthew 2:1), Joseph and Mary, His earthly parents, settled in the tiny town of Nazareth just west of the Sea of Galilee. That's where Jesus grew up. Working for Joseph in a carpenter's shop, Jesus' life was simple, quiet, and mostly uneventful until He was thirty. Then He began His public ministry. He lived thirty-three years—the first thirty in obscurity, the last three and a half in the limelight.

Upon entering the public arena, Jesus chose twelve Jewish men as His disciples (Luke 6:13–16) and taught vast multitudes that seemed irresistibly drawn to His goodness (Matthew 4:23–5:1). His favorite teaching method was to tell stories called "parables." In teaching spiritual truths, Jesus told parables about farmers, seeds, and harvests (Matthew 13:1–9, 24–30), hidden treasure (Matthew 13:44–52), lost sheep (Luke 15:4–7), missing coins (Luke 15:8–10), a wayward son (Luke 15:11–32), a wedding prepared by a king (Matthew 22:1–14), and ten virgins in a bridal party, five of whom weren't prepared to meet the bridegroom (Matthew 25:1–13). It's safe to say that Jesus Christ was the greatest storyteller the world has ever witnessed. His lessons were simple, yet profound, and the crowds that followed Him, composed of rich and poor alike, hung on His words. I did too when I first read these stories.

This Man from Nazareth made unique claims about Himself—claims no other human teacher ever made, including Socrates, Plato, Confucius, Buddha, and Mohammed. For instance, Jesus told an outcast Samaritan woman drawing water from a well, " 'Whoever drinks of this water will thirst again, but whoever drinks of the water that I shall give him will never thirst. But the water that I shall give him will become in him a fountain of water springing up into everlasting life' " (John 4:13, 14, emphasis added). A Man who could supply water bubbling up into everlasting life? This was unique. But so was what He said to a group of Jews who were wondering whether this unusual Galilean

Teacher might be Israel's true Messiah. " *'I am the bread of life,'* " He said. " 'He who comes to Me shall never hunger, and he who believes in Me shall never thirst' " (John 6:35, emphasis added).

To those familiar with flocks, shepherds, and sheep, Jesus declared, " *'I am the good shepherd.* . . . My sheep hear My voice, and I know them, and they follow Me. And I give them eternal life, and they shall never perish; neither shall anyone snatch them out of My Father's hand' " (John 10:14, 27, 28, emphasis added).

To a family mourning the loss of a loved one, He—shockingly!—stated, " *'I am the resurrection and the life.* He who believes in Me, though he may die, he shall live. And whoever lives and believes in Me shall never die. Do you believe this?' " (John 11:25, 26, emphasis added).

To His inner circle, He even announced, " *'I am the way, the truth, and the life.* No one comes to the Father except through Me' " (John 14:6, emphasis added).

"The light of the world," "the bread of life," "the good shepherd," "the resurrection and the life," "the way, the truth, and the life"? Jesus even went so far as to say that He was the eternal Son of God walking around in human form (John 3:16; 17:5). Either these unique statements are true or they reflect the wacky imaginings of a deluded fanatic. Some say, "Jesus? He was a good man, but He wasn't the Son of God!" But think about it. If He wasn't the Son of God, then He wasn't really a good man at all, for He would have been a consummate deceiver. "Liar, lunatic, or Lord," someone once said. He must be one or the other.

Jesus Christ didn't just tell intriguing stories and make claims. He did more. Matthew, Mark, Luke, and John all testify of His miracle-working power, especially toward those who were suffering. Reports like this are common: "Jesus went about all Galilee, teaching in their synagogues, preaching the gospel of the kingdom, and healing all kinds of sickness and all kinds of disease among the people. Then His fame went throughout all Syria; and they brought to Him all sick people who were afflicted with various diseases and torments, and those who were demon-possessed, epileptics, and paralytics; and He healed them. Great multitudes followed Him—from Galilee, and from Decapolis, Jerusalem, Judea, and beyond Jordan" (Matthew 4:23–25).

Jesus healed the sick, made cripples walk, unstopped the ears of the deaf, and opened the eyes of the blind. And if that isn't enough to validate His claims of heavenly origin, the Nazarene even exercised authority over humanity's greatest enemy—death. Standing before a rock-hewn tomb and speaking to the relative of the person lying dead within, Jesus said, " 'Did I not say to you that if you would believe you would see the glory of God?' Then they took away the stone from the place where the dead man was lying. And Jesus lifted up His eyes and said, 'Father, I thank You that You have heard Me. And I know that You always hear Me, but because of the people who are standing by I said this, that they may believe that You sent Me.' Now when He had said these things, He cried with a loud voice, 'Lazarus, come forth!' And he who had died came out bound hand and foot with graveclothes, and his face was wrapped with a cloth. Jesus said to them, 'Loose him, and let him go' " (John 11:40–44).

So, even death itself couldn't resist His power. Neither could demons. In those days, cases of devil possession were frequent. More than once the New Testament writers reported nightmarish scenes in which "unclean spirits" inhabiting unfortunate humans snarled viciously at Christ, challenged His authority, and sought to divert attention from His teachings. During each encounter with these malicious invisible entities, the Deliverer emerged victorious. The prophet Isaiah predicted that when Israel's Messiah came, He would set the captives free (see Isaiah 61:1; Luke 4:16–21). *The carpenter's Son did just that.*

Here's another account:

Then they went into Capernaum, and immediately on the Sabbath He entered the synagogue and taught. And they were astonished at His teaching, for He taught them as one having authority, and not as the scribes.

Now there was a man in their synagogue with an unclean spirit. And he cried out, saying, "Let *us* alone! What have we to do with You, Jesus of Nazareth? Did You come to destroy us? I know who You are—the Holy One of God!"

But Jesus rebuked him, saying, "Be quiet, and come out of him!" And when the unclean spirit had convulsed him and cried out with a loud voice, he came out of him. Then they were all amazed, so that they questioned among themselves, saying, "What is this? What new doctrine is this? For with authority He commands even the unclean spirits, and they obey Him." And immediately His fame spread throughout all the region around Galilee (Mark 1:21–28).

Uncontrollable forces of nature were also subject to Him. One night His disciples almost drowned when a storm caught them while they were crossing a lake. Mark reported, "When they had left the multitude, they took Him along in the boat as He was. And other little boats were also with Him. And a great windstorm arose, and the waves beat into the boat, so that it was already filling. But He was in the stern, asleep on a pillow. And they awoke Him and said to Him, 'Teacher, do You not care that we are perishing?'

"Then He arose and rebuked the wind, and said to the sea, 'Peace, be still!' And the wind ceased and there was a great calm. But He said to them, 'Why are you so fearful? How is it that you have no faith?' And they feared exceedingly, and said to one another, 'Who can this be, that even the wind and the sea obey Him!' " (Mark 4:36–41).

The Desire of Ages illuminates every scene exactly as depicted in the Bible. As I turned each page with fascinated interest, it became quite clear to me that the Person I was reading about was more than just a man. His claims, parables, miracles, and even His authority over devils and storms all resulted in a deepening conviction that He was who He claimed to be: God's own Son in human form.

Some reading this may be thinking, *Steve Wohlberg, you are so gullible! Do you believe everything you read in a book?* No; far from it. But the biblical account of the life of Jesus Christ differs vastly from the record of any other life. Through reading *The Desire of Ages* and the New Testament, I discovered that many in Christ's own day questioned His teachings, doubted His claims, rejected His message, considered Him dangerous, and were determined to silence Him. One time a group of hostile religious leaders sent an official delegation to arrest Christ as an imposter and bring Him to trial. But the delegation returned empty-handed. Why? Read it yourself: "Then the officers came to the chief priests and Pharisees, who said to them, 'Why have you not brought Him?' The officers answered, 'No man ever spoke like this Man!' " (John 7:45, 46).

"No one ever spoke like this Man!" That's exactly the way I felt. Yet something greater than wise words and control over devils and surging waves spoke to my heart. Something beyond magnificently crafted parables, supernatural healings, and even the ability to raise a rotting corpse back to life, as impressive as these were. It was His character: the patience, tenderness, and constant kindness that the Man from Nazareth revealed toward sinful, guilt-ridden men and women, both Jews and non-Jews—even to those who were bent on destroying Him. His *love* was drawing me, slowly, relentlessly, irresistibly.

This may surprise those familiar with the Bible, but after reading through chapters one through seventy-three in *The Desire of Ages,* I was still unclear about what would happen to Him at the end of those three and a half years of public ministry.

I was about to find out.

10

Garden
of Sorrows

"Trembling with fear, alone in the garden
Battle before the final war
Blood became tears, there in the garden
To fall upon the silent stone."
~ *"In the Garden" lyrics by Michael Card (1957–),*
award-winning American singer

Jesus' public ministry brought help to the helpless, hope to the hopeless, comfort to outcasts, forgiveness to the guilty, light to those in darkness, love to the lost— even life to the dead. But for some strange reason His works of mercy also generated hostility from certain religious leaders. They despised His purity, envied His power, and felt threatened by His growing popularity. Immediately after the resurrection of Lazarus, top Jewish officials "plotted to put Him to death" (John 11:53). Ancient prophecies were pending. His time was running out.

As I followed the story, dormitory life faded in importance for me. Although I had never been much of a reader, I had plowed through seventy-three beefy chapters of *The Desire of Ages* in a short time. Chapter seventy-four's mysterious title was simply "Gethsemane."

Gethsemane is an olive orchard that remains to this day just east of Jerusalem. Late on Thursday night during the season of the Jewish Passover, Jesus and His band of disciples were inside a Jerusalem residence. They had just finished eating the Passover meal commemorating Israel's deliverance from Egyptian bondage. Unknown to the city of slumbering pilgrims, another deliverance was at hand. Just before midnight, Jesus and the disciples left the city. *The Desire of Ages* reports, "In company with His disciples, the Saviour slowly made His way to the garden of Gethsemane. The Passover moon, broad and full, shone from a cloudless sky. The city of pilgrims' tents was hushed into silence.

"Jesus had been earnestly conversing with His disciples and instructing them; but as He neared Gethsemane, He became strangely silent. He had often visited this spot for meditation and prayer; but never with a heart so full of sorrow as upon this night of His last agony."[1]

Gethsemane—mysterious garden of sorrows. Little did I realize, as in my imagination I mentally approached its stately olive trees, that the bloodstained struggle that took place there would alter my life forever.

Jesus and His friends walked quietly toward His usual place of prayer. But something was different that night. An unseen pressure weighed heavily upon Jesus' heart. In less than twenty-four hours, He would be dead.

"As they approached the garden, the disciples had marked the change that came over their Master. Never before had they seen Him so utterly sad and silent. As He proceeded, this strange sadness deepened; yet they dared not question Him as to the cause. His form swayed as if He were about to fall. Upon reaching the garden, the disciples looked anxiously for His usual place of retirement, that their Master might rest. Every step that He now took was with labored effort. He groaned aloud, as if suffering under the pressure of a terrible burden. Twice His companions supported Him, or He would have fallen to the earth."[2]

The New Testament states simply, "Then Jesus came with them to a place called Gethsemane, and said to the disciples, 'Sit here while I go and pray over there.' And He took with Him Peter and the two sons of Zebedee, and He began to be sorrowful and deeply distressed. Then He said to them, 'My soul is exceedingly sorrowful, even to death. Stay here and watch with Me' " (Matthew 26:36–38).

Before taking Peter, James, and John deeper among the olive trees, Jesus left eight of His disciples at Gethsemane's entrance, instructing them to pray for Him. (Judas was absent, but not for long.) Continuing alone, Jesus went even farther into the inner recesses of the Garden to pray as He had never prayed before. *The Desire of Ages* comments, "He went a little distance from them—not so far but that they could both see and hear Him—and fell prostrate upon the ground. He felt that by sin He was being separated from His Father. The gulf was so broad, so black, so deep, that His spirit shuddered before it. This agony He must not exert His divine power to escape. As man He must suffer the consequences of man's sin. As man He must endure the wrath of God against transgression."[3]

The internal agony Jesus Christ experienced inside the Garden of Gethsemane surprised me and touched me deeply. If you could have seen my face, you would have seen an expression of bewilderment. *What's happening here?* I asked myself. *Why the trauma and pain?*

The paragraph I just quoted answered my question. "As man He must suffer the consequences of man's sin. As man He must endure the wrath of God against transgression." Jesus had also provided the answer, but He did so in terms that are cryptic and hard to comprehend. Moments before entering Gethsemane, He told His disciples, " 'All of you will be made to stumble because of Me this night, for it is written: "I will strike the Shepherd, and the sheep of the flock will be scattered" ' " (Matthew 26:31). Here Jesus quoted Zechariah 13:7, an Old Testament prophecy describing the future suffering of Israel's Messiah. The entire verse reads, " 'Awake, O sword, against My Shepherd, against the Man who is My Companion,' says the Lord of hosts. 'Strike the Shepherd, and the sheep will be scattered' " (Zechariah 13:7).

A careful reading of this verse reveals that God Himself ("the Lord of hosts") would at some point in human history command the unsheathing of a "sword" against His Shepherd, "the Man who is My Companion." In Matthew 26:31, Christ applied this prophecy to Himself—to the agony He was beginning to endure among the olive trees. The original prophecy in Zechariah 13:7 even stated, "Strike the Shepherd." With deep spiritual discernment, the writer of *The Desire of Ages* applied these cryptic phrases about a sword and striking the Shepherd to the unleashing of God's justice against the sin of the entire world, which, during one unfathomable twenty-four-hour period starting in Gethsemane, would mysteriously be transferred into the heart of His Son, who had consented to bear it. Sin within Christ and God's wrath on sin—that was the plan. The salvation of every person on planet Earth depended on Christ's willingness to go through with it.

"As the substitute and surety for sinful man, Christ was suffering under divine justice. He saw what justice meant. Hitherto He had been as an intercessor for others; now He longed to have an intercessor for Himself. . . . The conflict was terrible. Its measure was the guilt of His nation, of His accusers and betrayer, the guilt of a world lying in wickedness. The sins of men weighed heavily upon Christ, *and the sense of God's wrath against sin was crushing out His life.*"[4]

I could hardly comprehend what I was reading. The message

was much bigger than the book. Yet what first confused me slowly made sense—and this is where a real miracle occurred. In spite of my drug use, addictions, selfishness, and overall spiritual deadness, I, Steve Wohlberg, secular Jew and consummate pleasure-lover, *started understanding God's Word.* Rays of divine light penetrated my darkened mind. An unseen Power stood by my side right there in my CSUN dorm room. I lost track of time, of everything. All I saw was the Gethsemane Man. Alone in a garden. Suffering for me.

Human words can't fully reveal the issues. Matthew simply wrote, "He went a little farther and fell on His face, and prayed, saying, 'O My Father, if it is possible, let this cup pass from Me; nevertheless, not as I will, but as You will' " (Matthew 26:39).

As I've said many times, my father and I have always been close. In retrospect, I think this made it easier for the Spirit of the heavenly Father to move my heart. This is not to say that God can't perform mighty miracles inside those who don't have affectionate relationships with their parents. However, I believe it helped me. Here was a Son painfully praying to His Father, wrestling over whether or not to drink a deadly potion bubbling up inside a mystical "cup."

That cup was obviously symbolic, for the Gethsemane Man wasn't holding a literal cup in His hands. "Drinking the cup" meant swallowing the poison of every human being's sin. It meant enduring God's infinite justice against evil. Worst of all, it meant separation from His Father. And the Father and the Son loved each other. They had been together in eternity before Christ became Man. Earlier, Jesus told His enemies, " 'I and My Father are one' " (John 10:30). Now He contemplated separation. His whole being abhorred the thought. As Michael Card's song says, "Two choices, one tortured will." Yet He must make a choice: Drink the cup or watch us perish in our sins. That was His divine dilemma.

Choosing words that plunged deep inside me, the writer of *The Desire of Ages* appealed passionately, "Behold Him contemplating the price to be paid for the human soul. In His agony He clings to the cold ground, as if to prevent Himself from being drawn farther from God. The chilling dew of night falls upon His prostrate form, but He heeds it not. From His pale lips comes the bitter cry, 'O My Father, if it be possible, let this cup pass from Me.' Yet even now He adds, 'Nevertheless not as I will, but as Thou wilt.' "5

Hoping His disciples were praying, Jesus rose from the earth and staggered to the place where He had left them. But sadly, He "found them asleep" (Matthew 26:40). " 'What?' " Christ asked Peter, " 'Could you not watch with Me one hour? Watch and pray, lest you enter into temptation. The spirit indeed is willing, but the flesh is weak' " (Matthew 26:40, 41). What a merciful Messiah! Instead of condemning His drowsy disciples for failing Him during the hour of His greatest need, He mourned their weakness and urged them to awake and pray.

"Again the Son of God was seized with superhuman agony, and fainting and exhausted, He staggered back to the place of His former struggle. His suffering was even greater than before. As the agony of soul came upon Him, 'His sweat was as it were great drops of blood falling down to the ground.' The cypress and palm trees were the silent witnesses of His anguish. From their leafy branches dropped heavy dew upon His stricken form, as if nature wept over its Author wrestling alone with the powers of darkness."6

The Bible records that after Christ left His sleepy companions, "Again, a second time, He went away and prayed, saying, *'O My Father,* if this cup cannot pass away from Me unless I drink it, Your will be done' " (Matthew 26:42, emphasis added). There was that Father–Son struggle again. What a decision for Christ to face! Saving us meant bearing our sins, and bearing our sins meant separation from the One He loved most.

Retracing His steps, Jesus again went back to His disciples. What did He find? "He came and found them asleep again, for their eyes were heavy. So He left them, went away again, and prayed the third time, saying the same words" (Matthew 26:43, 44).

Watching Jesus agonize over this decision and pray the same prayer three times not only impressed me with His love for me, but it also showed me that I too had a choice to make. "Not My will, but Your will be done," Jesus said over and over again. His choice involved nothing less than absolute, 100 percent, and unquestioning submission to God's will. Slowly, I realized *so did my choice.* At this point, I had been reading the Bible for about two months and had even repeated the sinner's prayer in the home of a Baptist minister. But I had not completely or intelligently believed in Jesus as my personal Savior or surrendered myself to Him without reservation. Not yet. But the Holy Spirit, working through a book chapter titled "Gethsemane," was steadily moving me toward the point of no return.

Six consecutive paragraphs near the end of chapter seventy-four brought me over the line. They contain the heart of this book. Before reproducing them below, I must say that God used something else during those weighty moments to capture my heart fully. The edition of *The Desire of Ages* that I was reading contained two pictures of Jesus suffering among the olive trees. I know they are just artists' conceptions, for no one knows exactly what Christ looked like. But they worked for me. The first illustration is a full-page spread of Jesus looking terribly sad, with an angel standing behind Him and touching His shoulder. The second, directly opposite those six paragraphs, showed Him kneeling on a rock with one hand on the ground and the other over His heart. The pictures helped me visualize the reality of things unseen.

Even more important than their influence, however, was that of the eternal Spirit of the eternal Father. He revealed to my awe-struck mind the magnitude of the eternal Son's incomprehensible choice in the garden of sorrows.

Now, say a prayer. Here are those meaningful paragraphs:

Turning away [from His sleeping disciples], Jesus sought again His retreat, and fell prostrate, overcome by the horror of a great darkness. The humanity of the Son of God trembled in that trying hour. He prayed not now for His disciples that their faith might not fail, but for His own tempted, agonized soul. The awful moment had come—that moment which was to decide the destiny of the world. The fate of humanity trembled in the balance. Christ might even now refuse to drink the cup apportioned to guilty man. It was not yet too late. He might wipe the bloody sweat from His brow, and leave man to perish in his iniquity. He might say, Let the transgressor receive the penalty of his sin, and I will go back to My Father. Will the Son of God drink the bitter cup of humiliation and agony? Will the innocent suffer the consequences of the curse of sin, to save the guilty? The words fall tremblingly from the pale lips of Jesus, "O My Father, if this cup may not pass away from Me, except I drink it, Thy will be done."

Three times has He uttered that prayer. Three times has humanity shrunk from the last, crowning sacrifice. But now the history of the human race comes up before the world's Redeemer. He sees that the transgressors of the law, if left to themselves, must perish. He sees the helplessness of man. He sees the power of sin. The woes and lamentations of a doomed world rise before Him. He beholds its impending fate, and His decision is made. He will save man at any cost to Himself. He accepts His baptism of blood, that through

Him perishing millions may gain everlasting life. He has left the courts of heaven, where all is purity, happiness, and glory, to save the one lost sheep, the one world that has fallen by transgression. And He will not turn from His mission. He will become the propitiation of a race that has willed to sin. His prayer now breathes only submission: "If this cup may not pass away from Me, except I drink it, Thy will be done."

Having made the decision, He fell dying to the ground from which He had partially risen. Where now were His disciples, to place their hands tenderly beneath the head of their fainting Master, and bathe that brow, marred indeed more than the sons of men? The Saviour trod the wine press alone, and of the people there was none with Him.

But God suffered with His Son. Angels beheld the Saviour's agony. They saw their Lord enclosed by legions of satanic forces, His nature weighed down with a shuddering, mysterious dread. There was silence in heaven. No harp was touched. Could mortals have viewed the amazement of the angelic host as in silent grief they watched the Father separating His beams of light, love, and glory from His beloved Son, they would better understand how offensive in His sight is sin.

The worlds unfallen and the heavenly angels had watched with intense interest as the conflict drew to its close. Satan and his confederacy of evil, the legions of apostasy, watched intently this great crisis in the work of redemption. The powers of good and evil waited to see what answer would come to Christ's thrice-repeated prayer. Angels had longed to bring relief to the divine sufferer, but this might not be. No way of escape was found for the Son of God. In this awful crisis, when everything was at stake, when the mysterious cup trembled in the hand of the sufferer, the heavens opened, a light shone forth amid the stormy darkness of the crisis hour, and the mighty angel who stands in God's presence, occupying the position from which Satan fell, came to the side of Christ. The angel came not to take the cup from Christ's hand, but to strengthen Him to drink it, with the assurance of the Father's love. He came to give power to the divine-human suppliant. He pointed Him to the open heavens, telling Him of the souls that would be saved as the result of His sufferings. He assured Him that His Father is greater and more powerful than Satan, that His death would result in the utter discomfiture of Satan, and that the kingdom of this world would be given to the saints of the Most High. He told Him that He would see of the travail of His soul, and be satisfied, for He would see a multitude of the human race saved, eternally saved.

Christ's agony did not cease, but His depression and discouragement left Him. The storm had in nowise abated, but He who was its object was strengthened to meet its fury. He came forth calm and serene. A heavenly peace rested upon His bloodstained face. He had borne that which no human being could ever bear; for He had tasted the sufferings of death for every man.[7]

That did it. In the light of Christ's painful choice to endure separation from His Father, to bear the uncompromising "sword" of God's righteous justice against all sin, and to "taste death for everyone" (Hebrews 2:9), I lost all interest in marijuana, flashing discos, and Budweiser. My mind had just been taken into the heart of the New Testament, into the heart of heaven's pain, into the heart of God. That revelation smashed every barrier down. Even before I finished chapter seventy-four, my heart crossed the great divide. I now wanted Him more than I wanted anything else—more than life itself.

When I was five years old, Mike and I went fishing with Dad near the beautiful coastal town of Coronado, California. As I've said, fishing trips are some of my fondest childhood memories. But not that one. Unexpectedly, my appendix ruptured, which, back in those days, was life-threatening. My parents raced me to a local hospital, and I was rushed into a waiting chamber near an operating room.

To this day, I remember what happened next. My dad held me as I writhed in pain in his arms. Then a stranger wearing a mask walked over and started pulling me away from my father. "No! No! No! I don't want to go!" I screamed in terror as my little hands clung desperately to my dad's neck. But go I must. With terrible difficulty—difficulty only a father can fully understand—my dad slowly peeled each of my tiny fingers off his neck so that the strange man could take me away. "That was one of the hardest moments in my entire life," my dad told me later.

Why was I ripped out of my father's arms? So the doctor could remove my appendix and save my life. On an infinitely greater scale, that's exactly what happened to Jesus Christ in Gethsemane and on the cross. He was separated from His Father.

They did it to save our souls.

---

1. Ellen G. White, *The Desire of Ages* (Nampa, Idaho: Pacific Press®, 1940), 685.

2. Ibid., 685, 686.

3. Ibid., 686.

4. Ibid., 686, 687; emphasis added.

5. Ibid., 687.

6. Ibid., 689.

7. Ibid., 690–694.

11

Midnight
Trials

"Conflict builds character. Crisis defines it."
~ Steven V. Thulon

Chapters seventy-five through eighty-seven of *The Desire of Ages* zoom in on the closing scenes of the earthly life of One who claimed to be the Son of God. I read *The Desire of Ages* and the Bible together. They fit perfectly.

Right after Christ's spiritual battle in Gethsemane, His thrice-repeated prayer, and His final choice to endure separation from His Father, "Judas, one of the twelve," showed up at the gate of the Garden "with a great multitude with swords and clubs, [sent] from the chief priests and elders of the people" (Matthew 26:47). "Judas" is the name of one of history's most infamous characters. Countless babies are named after David, Ruth, Esther, Daniel, Matthew, Mark, Luke, John, Mary, James, Peter, and Paul—all well-known Bible characters. But few parents name their children Judas. The reason is simple: Judas betrayed Jesus Christ.

Numerous books have been written about the injustices the Nazarene endured after His Gethsemane conflict. I won't attempt to describe every detail. Suffice it to say that the scenes are intense and high-powered, and that millions throughout history, including me, have been transformed by reading them. Whatever your opinion of Mel Gibson's 2004 movie *The Passion of the Christ,* that movie has taken its place as one of the biggest box office hits of all time. Its focus was those very events. So, it is obvious that what occurred from Gethsemane to the Crucifixion still speaks to human hearts today—big time.

Every major movie studio rejected Gibson's film, so he produced it on his own and with his own money. Hollywood spurned it, yet the masses flocked to theaters to watch it. Something similar happened two thousand years ago: the establishment rejected Jesus Christ.

When Judas secretly betrayed his Master to religious leaders thirsty for His blood, rowdy men with unfeeling hearts arrested Jesus and whisked Him back to Jerusalem. It was now past midnight. Those men should have been sleeping at home with their families. But no, they had work to do—not an ounce of which was honest, fair, or right. After all, if their cause was just, why have a trial at 2 A.M.? As Jesus' hands were being securely tied with ropes, He spoke with dignity "to the chief priests, captains of the temple, and the elders who had come to Him, 'Have you come out, as against a robber, with swords and clubs? When I was with you daily in the temple, you did not try to seize Me.' " Then He added sorrowfully, " 'But this is your hour, and the power of darkness' " (Luke 22:52, 53).

A cruel sequence of trials followed. Jesus was taken before the Jewish Sanhedrin, before Pontius Pilate, governor of Judea, the ruler with the highest position in the region, then before a profligate Judean king named Herod, and finally before Pilate again. The New Testament faithfully records highlights of each judicial session. Standing innocent before corrupt earthly judges and bribed false accusers, most of the time "Jesus kept silent" and said nothing (Matthew 26:63). But then the Jewish high priest,

Caiaphas, commanded, " 'I put You under oath by the living God: Tell us if you are the Christ, the Son of God!' " (Matthew 26:63).

It was time to tell the truth. With words that burned like fire, "Jesus said to him, 'It is as you said. Nevertheless, I say to you, hereafter you will see the Son of Man sitting at the right hand of the Power, and coming on the clouds of heaven' " (Matthew 26:64).

Silence pervaded the assembly. Christ's hearers were stunned. Quaking under conviction, Caiaphas nevertheless screamed out, "Blasphemy!" and condemned Jesus to death. Because under Roman rule the Jews had no authority to execute people, "the chief priests and elders of the people" led Christ away "and delivered Him to Pontius Pilate the governor" (Matthew 27:1, 2).

Awakened early by Jewish officials and an angry mob that dragged in an unknown prisoner, Pilate was not in a good mood. "Why are you here at this miserable hour?" he demanded.

" 'We found this fellow perverting the nation, ' " Caiaphas responded, " 'saying that He Himself is Christ, a King' " (Luke 23:2)! The high priest hoped his accusation that Jesus claimed to be a king would spur Pilate on to condemn Him as a threat to Caesar.

The Desire of Ages describes the scene: "Pilate looked at the men who had Jesus in charge, and then his gaze rested searchingly on Jesus. He had had to deal with all kinds of criminals; but never before had a man bearing marks of such goodness and nobility been brought before him. On His face he saw no sign of guilt, no expression of fear, no boldness or defiance. He saw a man of calm and dignified bearing, whose countenance bore not the marks of a criminal, but the signature of heaven."[1]

Pilate was deeply impressed. His better nature was aroused. Looking upon Christ and noting the purity of His countenance, he quickly assumed that a plot had been hatched against an innocent man. While not having the reputation of being a conscientious judge, Pilate nevertheless shrank from condemning someone who appeared so noble. So, he decided to interview his unusual prisoner privately. The New Testament reports the following dramatic dialogue:

> Then Pilate entered the Praetorium again, called Jesus, and said to Him, "Are You the king of the Jews?"
>
> Jesus answered him, "Are you speaking for yourself about this, or did others tell you this about Me?"
>
> Pilate answered, "Am I a Jew? Your own nation and the chief priests have delivered You to me. What have You done?"
>
> Jesus answered, "My kingdom is not of this world. If My kingdom were of this world, My servants would fight, so that I should not be delivered to the Jews; but now My kingdom is not from here."
>
> Pilate therefore said to Him, "Are You a king then?" Jesus answered, "You say rightly that I am a king. For this cause I was born, and for this cause I have come into the world, that I should bear witness to the truth. Everyone who is of the truth hears My voice."
>
> Pilate said to Him, "What is truth?" And when he had said this, he went out again to the Jews, and said to them, "I find no fault in Him at all" (John 18:33–38).

Pilate was deeply impressed. Unwilling to pronounce sentence upon One claiming such a close connection with heaven, Pilate returned to the clamoring mob and declared, "I find no fault in Him at all."

This was *not* what the crowd wanted to hear. Becoming unruly, they demanded Christ's blood. Sensing that their prey might escape, crafty religious rulers desperately threw Pilate a curveball, shouting, " 'If you let this Man go, you are not Caesar's friend. Whoever makes himself a king speaks against Caesar' " (John 19:12). This struck Pilate below the belt. His loyalty to Caesar was already under suspicion, and if more doubts reached Rome, he could be marked for execution.

> Pilate said to them, "What then shall I do with Jesus who is called Christ?" They all said to him, "Let Him be crucified!"
>
> Then the governor said, "Why, what evil has He done?" But they cried out all the more, saying, "Let Him be crucified!"
>
> When Pilate saw that he could not prevail at all, but rather that a tumult was rising, he took water and washed his hands before the multitude, saying, "I am innocent of the blood of this just Person. You see to it."
>
> And all the people answered and said, "His blood be on us and on our children." . . . And when he [Pilate] had scourged Jesus, he delivered Him to be crucified (Matthew 27:22–26).

This dialogue will remain on record until the end of time. Here a Roman governor, supposedly the guardian of justice, under intense pressure from a bloodthirsty mob finally consented to sacrifice an innocent man in order to preserve his job and possibly his life. Jesus had committed no crime, yet He was handed over to rough Roman soldiers to be cruelly scourged and then crucified. That entire period, starting with the betrayal by Judas, through the midnight trials, beyond Pilate's bizarre pronouncement (which affirmed Jesus' innocence yet treated Him as guilty), to the whippings, and finally, to the Crucifixion, witnessed the greatest injustices ever perpetrated against One so pure and undeserving of punishment. Yet Jesus took everything patiently, without retaliation, with godlike dignity.

Utterly confused by this unexpected turn of events, Jesus' disciples lost all hope that He might be Israel's long-awaited Messiah. Yet none of this took Jesus by surprise. He commented, " 'All this was done that the Scriptures of the prophets might be fulfilled' " (Matthew 26:56).

Like the chapter titled "Gethsemane," the title of the next chapter in *The Desire of Ages* contained only one word: "Calvary." Alone in my dorm room, I turned the page.

---

1. Ellen G. White, *The Desire of Ages* (Nampa, Idaho: Pacific Press®, 1940), 724.

12

Place of
a Skull

"Down the Via Dolorosa called the Way of Suffering,
Like a lamb came the Messiah, Christ the King.
But He chose to walk that road
Out of his love for you and me.
Down the Via Dolorosa all the way to Calvary."
~lyrics from "Via Dolorosa,"
written by Billy Sprague and Niles Borop

In a sense, reading *The Desire of Ages* was like watching a movie—every scene was described clearly and dramatically. Surrounded by hardened Roman soldiers, devastated disciples, and sneering enemies, Jesus staggered out of Pilate's Roman headquarters, down the streets of Jerusalem and through a gate in the city's western wall, toward the appointed place of crucifixion. Blood flowed from deep welts in His back and from His head, where a circle of thorns had mockingly been placed upon His brow. Mel Gibson's film may have overdramatized the scene, or it may not have. No doubt, the scene was ugly.

"A vast multitude followed Jesus from the judgment hall to Calvary. The news of His condemnation had spread throughout

Jerusalem, and people of all classes and all ranks flocked toward the place of crucifixion."[1]

Once outside the city, soldiers thrust a splintery cross upon His back and other crosses upon the shoulders of two thieves who were condemned to die with Him. Although Jesus was the Prince of sufferers, the weight of the heavy wood became too much for even Him to bear. He collapsed under the pressure. My book reported,

> The Saviour's burden was too heavy for Him in His weak and suffering condition. Since the Passover supper with His disciples, He had taken neither food nor drink. He had agonized in the garden of Gethsemane in conflict with satanic agencies. He had endured the anguish of the betrayal, and had seen His disciples forsake Him and flee. He had been taken to Annas, then to Caiaphas, and then to Pilate. From Pilate He had been sent to Herod, then sent again to Pilate. From insult to renewed insult, from mockery to mockery, twice tortured by the scourge,—all that night there had been scene after scene of a character to try the soul of man to the uttermost. Christ had not failed. He had spoken no word but that tended to glorify God. All through the disgraceful farce of a trial He had borne Himself with firmness and dignity. But when after the second scourging the cross was laid upon Him, human nature could bear no more. He fell fainting beneath the burden.[2]

Never had such a scene been witnessed. Whether or not you believe He was the divine Son of God, these events have become the life-changing core of the faith of millions.

In the crowd that day were friends, enemies, curious onlookers, priests, temple guards, and scribes—all highly visible to human vision. Yet that day there were also other watchers who could not be seen—holy angels weeping, demons scowling, and the prince of darkness himself, who nervously wondered whether he was about to conquer or to be conquered. The security of the entire universe was at stake.

Jesus was now too weak to shoulder the cross, so grabbing "a man of Cyrene, Simon by name," the Roman soldiers compelled him to carry Jesus' cross (Matthew 27:32). The procession moved slowly onward and upward, toward the crest of a hill not far from Jerusalem. "And when they had come to the place called Calvary, there they crucified Him" (Luke 23:33). The spot was also named "Golgotha, which is translated, Place of a Skull" (Mark 15:22), because it sat upon a rock formation resembling a skull.

Upon reaching this site, soldiers thrust Jesus down on the wooden cross and drove spikes through His hands and feet. "With Him they also crucified two robbers, one on His right hand and the other on His left. So the Scripture was fulfilled which says, 'And He was numbered with the transgressors' " (Mark 15:27, 28). There He hung, the innocent between the guilty. It was about 9 A.M., Roman time.

Once, when I was a teenager, a friend named Darren spent the night at my house. We talked about how fortunate we were to have never broken a bone in our bodies. The next day, we swung from a rope tied to the top of a tree in the Hollywood Hills. Darren slipped off the rope and slammed hard into the ground. When he stood up and raised his right arm, it was twisted like a pretzel. I still remember his terrified scream echoing among the oak trees as he collapsed in excruciating pain. What did crucifixion feel like? We'll never know.

Jesus hung upon a cross for six dreadful hours. Almost every sound that reached His ears was unpleasant. Mark wrote, "Those who passed by blasphemed Him, wagging their heads and saying, 'Aha! You who destroy the temple and build it again in three days, save Yourself, and come down from the cross!' Likewise the chief priests also, mocking among themselves with the scribes, said, 'He saved others; Himself He cannot save. Let the Christ, the King of Israel, descend now from the cross, that we may see and believe.' Even those who were crucified with Him reviled Him" (Mark 15:29–32).

According to the Bible, what happened that day meant much more than spurting blood and the physical agony of an innocent Man nailed onto a wooden cross above a skull-shaped hill. Beyond the tumult of angry voices, *"the Scripture was fulfilled"* (Mark 15:28, emphasis added). Though mocking priests and rulers didn't realize it, prophecy after ancient prophecy met fulfillment before their very eyes. If you are wrestling with the Book's credibility, let this strengthen your faith:

1. **His birth:** As we have already seen, the Bible says, "Jesus was born in Bethlehem" (Matthew 2:1). Micah identified Bethlehem as the place of His birth seven hundred years before the event (see Micah 5:2).

2. **His herald:** Isaiah predicted that someone "crying in the wilderness" would " 'prepare the way of the Lord' " (Isaiah 40:3). John the Baptist, who lived and preached in the Judean wilderness, fulfilled this prophecy exactly. When questioned by religious leaders about his mission, John quoted Isaiah 40:3 (see Matthew 3:1–3).

3. **His tribe:** Jacob predicted that the Messiah (called "Shiloh") would rise out of Judah (see Genesis 49:10). Jesus Christ's earthly lineage went back to the tribe of Judah (see Luke 3:23–33).

4. **His triumphal entry:** Zechariah predicted that the Messiah would enter Jerusalem riding a donkey, like a

king (Zechariah 9:9). Jesus did just that (see Matthew 21:1–9). *"All this was done that it might be fulfilled which was spoken by the prophet"* (Matthew 21:4, emphasis added).

5. **His betrayer:** David described the Messiah's betrayal by a "familiar friend" who shared a meal with Him (see Psalm 41:9). Jesus applied this passage to Judas, one of His own disciples, who betrayed Him immediately after they shared the Passover meal (see Matthew 26:23–25).

6. **His price:** After describing the Messiah's entry into Jerusalem on a donkey, Zechariah predicted He would be betrayed for "thirty pieces of silver" (Zechariah 11:12). This money would be thrown "to the potter" (verse 13). Amazingly, Christ's enemies paid Judas *exactly* thirty pieces of silver for his notorious deed (see Matthew 26:14–16), and this money was later used to buy "the potter's field, to bury strangers in" (see Matthew 27:3–10)!

7. **His silence:** In one of the clearest Old Testament prophecies about the Messiah's sufferings, Isaiah not only predicted that He would be "despised and rejected by men" (Isaiah 53:3) but also that while "taken from prison and from judgment" (verse 8), "He opened not His mouth" (verse 7). This was strikingly fulfilled as the innocent Prisoner stood before the Sanhedrin, Herod, and Pontius Pilate (see Matthew 26:63; 27:12–14; Luke 23:8, 9).

8. **His companions:** Isaiah 53 predicted that at the time of the Messiah's "death," He would be "numbered with the transgressors" (verse 12). After Christ was condemned, "with Him they also crucified two robbers, one on His

right and the other on His left. *So the Scripture was fulfilled which says, 'And He was numbered with the transgressors'* " (Mark 15:27, 28, emphasis added).

9. **His crucifixion:** Zechariah also predicted, " 'they will look on Me whom they have pierced' " (Zechariah 12:10). The New Testament reports that right after Jesus died, as His lifeless body hung motionless between heaven and earth, *"the Scripture [was] fulfilled. . . . 'They shall look on Him whom they pierced'* " (John 19:36, 37, emphasis added).

10. **His burial:** Isaiah 53 predicted that after a period of great suffering, the Messiah would be buried "with the rich at His death" (verse 9). After Jesus died, "there came a rich man from Arimathea, named Joseph," who took Christ's body off the cross and "laid it in his new tomb which he had hewn out of the rock" (Matthew 27:57–60).

The Desire of Ages showed the fulfillment of each of these prophecies and many more.

Beyond the physical pain inflicted by fists, whips, thorns, splinters, and nails, Jesus Christ's greatest suffering was mental. An invisible horror entered His mind and broke His heart. The Bible says, "He was wounded for our transgressions, He was bruised for our iniquities; the chastisement for our peace was upon Him, and by His stripes we are healed. All we like sheep have gone astray; we have turned every one, to his own way; *and the Lord has laid on Him the iniquity of us all"* (Isaiah 53:5, 6, emphasis added).

This unlocks the mystery of the Cross. What began beneath olive trees climaxed above the Place of a Skull. As Christ's body hung between heaven and earth, "the iniquity

[sin] of us all" swirled inside His mind with deadlier force than any hurricane. After three hours of unimaginable torment, the eye of the storm reached the cross. Jesus' heart erupted in pain. Onlookers milling around Calvary were then shocked to hear "Jesus [cry] out with a loud voice, saying, 'Eli, Eli, lama sabachthani?' that is, 'My God, My God, why have You forsaken Me?' " (Matthew 27:46). If Christ's suffering were a hurricane, it was now a category 10.

The Desire of Ages reports, "The guilt of every descendant of Adam was pressing upon His heart. The wrath of God against sin, the terrible manifestation of His displeasure because of iniquity, filled the soul of His Son with consternation. All His life Christ had been publishing to a fallen world the good news of the Father's mercy and pardoning love. Salvation for the chief of sinners was His theme. But now with the terrible weight of guilt He bears, He cannot see the Father's reconciling face. The withdrawal of the divine countenance from the Saviour in this hour of supreme anguish pierced His heart with a sorrow that can never be fully understood by man. So great was this agony that His physical pain was hardly felt."[3]

This paragraph pierced me when I read it in my dorm room, and it pierces me now. We'll never fully understand that moment when Jesus felt forsaken by His Father, but we can try. As I write today, I'm now a father of a thirteen-month-old baby boy named Seth. My wife, Kristin, and I love him so much. Two days ago, something small happened, but it taught me a big lesson. Seth can't talk yet, so instead of calling me "Daddy," he says "Gagi." Because of my travels, I hadn't seen Kristin or Seth in five days. "Guess what Seth did when he woke up today?" Kristin asked as we talked on our cell phones. "He ran into your office and called, 'Gagi?' Then he hurried into the bathroom calling, 'Gagi?' Then he rushed into the bedroom saying, 'Gagi?' *He was searching for you, and you weren't there.*" This broke my heart.

I know the parallel breaks down in a zillion ways, but in a sense, the Son of God screamed "Gagi!" above the Place of a Skull, and no one answered. We can't comprehend His sorrow. Jesus not only felt that His Father wasn't there, but He felt that His Father had forsaken Him because He was bearing our sins inside Himself. Then a supernatural shadow fell suddenly on Calvary. "From the sixth hour until the ninth hour there was darkness over all the land" (Matthew 27:45). That darkness fell at noon on Friday afternoon and remained until 3 P.M., throughout Christ's last hours of suffering. As Jesus hung suspended on that shaft of wood between two thieves, a much deeper darkness enveloped His heart. *The Desire of Ages* describes Christ's expiring agony with these heart-breaking yet triumphant words:

> The spotless Son of God hung upon the cross, His flesh lacerated with stripes; those hands so often reached out in blessing, nailed to the wooden bars; those feet so tireless on ministries of love, spiked to the tree; that royal head pierced by the crown of thorns; those quivering lips shaped to the cry of woe. And all that He endured— the blood drops that flowed from His head, His hands, His feet, the agony that racked His frame, and the unutterable anguish that filled His soul at the hiding of His Father's face—speaks to each child of humanity, declaring, It is for thee that the Son of God consents to bear this burden of guilt; for thee He spoils the domain of death, and opens the gates of Paradise. He who stilled the angry waves and walked the foam-capped billows, who made devils tremble and disease flee, who opened blind eyes and called forth the dead to life,—offers Himself upon the cross as a sacrifice, and this from love to thee. He, the Sin Bearer, endures the wrath of divine justice, and for thy sake becomes sin itself. . . .

Suddenly the gloom lifted from the cross, and in clear, trumpet-like tones that seemed to resound throughout creation, Jesus cried, "It is finished" [John 19:30] "Father, into Thy hands I commend My spirit" [Luke 23:46]. A light encircled the cross, and the face of the Saviour shone with a glory like the sun. He then bowed His head upon His breast, and died.[4]

I was numb after reading this. Is that it? I wondered in shocked amazement. Believe it or not, I wasn't sure what would happen next. Even though Jesus Christ plainly predicted His resurrection numerous times during His public ministry, even His own disciples didn't get it. "They understood none of these things" (Luke 18:34). Neither did I.

Anxiously, I turned the page.

---

1. Ellen G. White, *The Desire of Ages* (Nampa, Idaho: Pacific Press®, 1940), 741.
2. Ibid., 741, 742.
3. Ibid., 753.
4. Ibid., 755, 756.

13

An Empty Tomb

"Darkness cannot drive
out darkness; only light can do that."
~ Martin Luther King Jr. (1929–1968),
American civil rights leader

For six dreadful hours, Christ suffered on the cross—until witnesses heard Him shout, " 'It is finished!' " (John 19:30). At that moment, "the earth quaked, and the rocks were split" (Matthew 27:51). Terror struck the priests, rulers, soldiers, scribes, and Pharisees gathered at the Place of a Skull. A Roman centurion, after seeing "the earthquake and the things that had happened . . . feared greatly, saying, 'Truly this was the Son of God!' " (Matthew 27:54). *He was right!*

Because the death of their Master wasn't what Christ's disciples expected, they lost all hope of His being Israel's true Messiah—yet they still longed to give Him an honorable burial. Then "Joseph, . . . a good and just man . . . went to Pilate and asked for the body of Jesus. Then he took it down, wrapped it in linen, and laid it in a tomb that was hewn out of the rock, where no one had ever lain before" (Luke 23:50–53). Christ was buried in Joseph's tomb, a cavernous hole cut into rock, and after mourners had paid their final respects, a heavy stone was rolled in front of its entrance. At last, the Sufferer was at rest—alone, lying in state, in pitch darkness, dead.

An unusual set of circumstances occurred after that stone was rolled into place. Christ's enemies exulted over the success of their plans, but their joy was short-lived. Back in Jerusalem, they pondered Christ's haunting statements about being "raised the third day" (Matthew 16:21). An irresistible nervousness settled over them—so much so that they wanted a guard posted outside Joseph's tomb!

Matthew reports, "On the next day, which followed the Day of Preparation, the chief priests and Pharisees gathered together to Pilate, saying, 'Sir, we remember, while He was still alive, how that deceiver said, "After three days I will rise." Therefore, command that the tomb be made secure until the third day, lest His disciples come by night and steal Him away, and say to the people, "He has risen from the dead." So the last deception will be worse than the first.' Pilate said to them, 'You have a guard; go your way, make it as secure as you know how.' So they went and made the tomb secure, sealing the stone and setting the guard" (Matthew 27:62–66).

Making "the tomb secure" meant sealing the stone with an official Roman seal; anyone who broke that seal would be subject to the death penalty. It also meant that soldiers would guard the tomb. However, the very measures taken by the priests and Pharisees to secure the body and thus destroy faith in Jesus only made what happened next more undeniable.[1] *The Desire of Ages* comments,

> So weak men counseled and planned. Little did these murderers realize the uselessness of their efforts. But by their action God was glorified. The very efforts made to prevent Christ's resurrection are the most convincing arguments in its proof. The greater the number of soldiers placed around the tomb, the stronger would be the testimony that

He had risen. Hundreds of years before the death of Christ, the Holy Spirit had declared through the psalmist, "Why do the heathen rage, and the people imagine a vain thing? The kings of the earth set themselves, and the rulers take counsel together, against the Lord, and against His anointed. . . . He that sitteth in the heavens shall laugh: the Lord shall have them in derision." Ps. 2:1-4. Roman guards and Roman arms were powerless to confine the Lord of life within the tomb. The hour of His release was near.[2]

"The hour of His release was near"! When I first read these words in the dorm, I also remembered how Jesus had told His disciples He would rise from the dead. Now I could feel it coming. Everyone knows that Hollywood films don't always have happy endings. *Titanic* didn't; the ship hit the ice, and most of its passengers drowned. At the height of the Cold War, a dismal production called *The Day After* concluded with the heroes rotting away from deadly radiation disease after a nuclear holocaust. But this would be different. After witnessing Gethsemane, Christ's betrayal, those midnight trials, and Calvary, I breathlessly turned pages toward an ending that wasn't fiction and that would change my life forever. The Preparation Day (Friday) merged into the Sabbath (see Luke 23:46–56). Then Saturday night slipped away and Sunday approached.

"The night of the first day of the week had worn slowly away. The darkest hour, just before daybreak, had come. Christ was still a prisoner in His narrow tomb. The great stone was in its place; the Roman seal was unbroken; the Roman guards were keeping their watch. And there were unseen watchers. Hosts of evil angels were gathered about the place. Had it been possible, the prince of darkness with his apostate army would have kept forever sealed the tomb that held the Son of God. But a heavenly host surrounded the sepulcher. Angels that excel in strength were guarding the tomb, and waiting to welcome the Prince of life."[3]

God's voice may have thundered from beyond the stars, "Gabriel—it's time!" Quicker than lightning, an unidentified flying object entered earth's atmosphere. Unseen by man, it soared with incalculable speed toward the Middle East, toward the land of Israel, toward the city of Jerusalem. Its target: a stone covering a tomb cut deep in rock. The Scripture records, "Behold, there was a great earthquake; for an angel of the Lord descended from heaven, and came and rolled back the stone from the door, and sat on it. His countenance was like lightning, and his clothing as white as snow. And the guards shook for fear of him, and became like dead men" (Matthew 28:2–4).

The Desire of Ages adds:

Now, priests and rulers, where is the power of your guard? Brave soldiers that have never been afraid of human power are now as captives taken without sword or spear. The face they look upon is not the face of mortal warrior; it is the face of the mightiest of the Lord's host. This messenger is he who fills the position from which Satan fell. It is he who on the hills of Bethlehem proclaimed Christ's birth. The earth trembles at his approach, the hosts of darkness flee, and as he rolls away the stone, heaven seems to come down to the earth. The soldiers see him removing the stone as he would a pebble, and hear him cry, Son of God, come forth; Thy Father calls Thee. They see Jesus come forth from the grave, and hear Him proclaim over the rent sepulcher, "I am the resurrection, and the life." As He comes forth in majesty and glory, the angel host bow low in adoration before the Redeemer, and welcome Him with songs of praise. . . .

Christ came forth from the tomb glorified, and the Roman guard beheld Him. Their eyes were riveted upon the face of Him whom they had so recently mocked and derided. In this glorified Being they beheld the prisoner whom they had seen in the judgment hall, the one for whom they had plaited a crown of thorns. This was the One who had stood unresisting before Pilate and Herod, His form lacerated by the cruel scourge. This was He who had been nailed to the cross, at whom the priests and rulers, full of self-satisfaction, had wagged their heads, saying, "He saved others; Himself He cannot save." Matt. 27:42. This was He who had been laid in Joseph's new tomb. The decree of heaven had loosed the captive. Mountains piled upon mountains over His sepulcher could not have prevented Him from coming forth.[4]

Jesus Christ was alive! Within minutes after the angel's descent, all that remained inside Joseph's tomb was a linen garment folded neatly where His body had lain. No more Roman seal, a covering stone, or tough Roman guard. The guards had staggered away like men who had seen a ghost. But as of yet, the depressed followers of the Savior knew none of this.

In words worth repeating to the close of time, the Bible describes what happened next: "Now when the Sabbath was past, Mary Magdalene, Mary the mother of James, and Salome bought spices, that they might come and anoint Him. Very early in the morning, on the first day of the week, they came to the tomb when the sun had risen. And they said among themselves, 'Who will roll away the stone from the door of the tomb for us?' But when they looked up, they saw that the stone had been rolled away—for it was very large. And entering the tomb, they saw a young man clothed in a long white robe sitting on the right side; and they were alarmed. But he said to them, 'Do not be alarmed. You seek Jesus of Nazareth, who was crucified. He is risen! He is not here. See the place where they laid Him' " (Mark 16:1–6, emphasis added).

"He is risen!" That's what the angel said. I could hardly believe it. It all seemed too good to be true. But it was true. How fantastic! In a short time I devoured the remaining chapters of *The*

Desire of Ages, which describe Christ's joyful reunion with His disciples (see John 20:19, 20), His command that they preach to all nations the good news of salvation (see Matthew 28:18), and His visible, bodily ascension back to heaven in full view of His awestruck followers.

The Bible says that forty days after His resurrection (see Acts 1:3), "while they [the disciples] watched, He was taken up, and a cloud received Him out of their sight. And while they looked steadfastly toward heaven as He went up, behold, two men stood by them in white apparel, who also said, 'Men of Galilee, why do you stand gazing up into heaven? This same Jesus, who was taken up from you into heaven, will so come in like manner as you saw Him go into heaven' " (Acts 1:9–11).

Those two men in shiny robes were angels in human form. Their message to the disciples was clear: Just as Jesus Christ was literally "taken up ... into heaven" after accomplishing His earthly mission, even so will He someday return "in like manner" as they "saw Him go into heaven." *Wow!* Angels sang at His birth near Bethlehem, and one rolled away the stone on the morning of His resurrection. Now, two more were announcing that He would return the same way He left. But we have more than simply angelic words to assure us of His return. The Savior promised, " '*I will come again* and receive you to Myself, that were I am, there you may be also' " (John 14:3, emphasis added).

After reading the final paragraph in the hardcover volume originally handed to me by an elderly man named Pastor Church, I closed the book.

---

1. For historical evidence of Christ's resurrection, see Josh McDowell's *The Resurrection Factor* (San Bernardino, Calif.: Here's Life Publishers, 1981).

2. Ellen G. White, *The Desire of Ages* (Nampa, Idaho: Pacific Press®, 1940), 778.

3. Ibid., 779.

4. Ibid., 779–781.

14

From Hollywood to Heaven

"Behold, I stand at the door and knock.
If anyone hears My voice and opens the door,
I will come in to him and dine with him,
And he with Me."
~ Jesus Christ, Revelation 3:20

There's a famous essay titled "One Solitary Life." Easily found in many forms on the World Wide Web, It highlights the incalculable effect the life of Jesus Christ continues to have upon humanity. Here it is:

He was born in an obscure village, the child of a peasant. He grew up in another village, where He worked in a carpenter shop until He was thirty. Then, for three years, He was an itinerant preacher.

He never wrote a book. He never held an office. He never had a family or owned a home. He didn't go to college. He never lived in a big city. He never traveled two hundred miles from the place where He was born. He did none of the things that usually accompany greatness. He had no credentials but Himself.

He was only thirty-three when the tide of public opinion turned against Him. His friends ran away. One of them denied Him. He was turned over to His enemies and went through the mockery of a trial. He was nailed to a cross between two thieves. While He was dying, His executioners gambled for His garments—the only property He had on earth. When He was dead, He was laid in a borrowed grave through the pity of a friend.

Nineteen centuries have come and gone, and today He is the central figure of the human race. I am well within the mark when I say that all the armies that ever marched, all the navies that ever sailed, all the parliaments that ever sat, all the kings that ever reigned—put together—have not affected the life of man on this earth as much as that one, solitary life.[1]

That essay is true. Twenty-six years ago, that truth reached me. I don't remember exactly what I was reading in *The Desire of Ages* when I did it or what day it was when I did it. But at some point, I slipped to my knees beside my bed in the CSUN dorm and said a little prayer.

For many of you reading this book, prayer is normal. If you grew up in a religious home, you've probably been praying most of your life—praying for yourself, for your family, to find lost car keys, to lose weight, to gain weight, for help with homework, about whom to date or marry, et cetera. Not me. My first twenty years were totally prayerless. "Pray? To whom?" You know that I repeated the sinner's prayer at Pastor Harper's home. Even then, however, I only said what he told me to say. This was different.

I don't remember my exact words, but they were something like "Dear God, I believe that Jesus Christ is Your Son, that He died for me on the cross and rose again. I've done a lot of bad things. I'm not worthy. But if You want me, if You'll take me, please forgive me and save me from my sins. In Jesus' name, amen."

My prayer was short, and as I said, I don't remember my exact words. But I do remember one thing as clearly as if I prayed this prayer just yesterday. It's the soothing sense of peace that instantly flowed into me. I had never felt anything quite like that before. *This is better than drugs!* I thought. Jesus told His disciples, " 'Peace I leave with you, *My peace I give to you;* not as the world gives do I give to you' " (John 14:27, emphasis added). I felt that peace. It was real. It entered me. It changed me.

At that moment, I experienced something else too. As we've already seen, on the morning of Christ's resurrection, a mighty angel descended from heaven and "rolled back the stone" from the mouth of the cave (Matthew 28:2). Right after my little prayer, something similar happened inside my head. The stone of guilt rolled away. And so did the heavy stones of drugs, alcohol, and slavery to nasty habits as a very real, supernatural Presence entered me. I was free! Psychologists may not comprehend it, skeptics may deny it, doubters deride it, and demons despise it—I don't care. *It happened to me,* and no human or devil can take it from me. Hollywood faded, and heaven moved in. I became a Jewish believer in Jesus Christ. *This is the truth.*

* * *

Normally, when I tell my story, I stop right here. But my publisher has suggested that I share a little more about what God has done since He rolled away the stones in my life and switched me from rock 'n' roll to the Rock of Ages. Because of this request, I'm now going to write some things I've never shared publicly in any presentation.

"Marketing is out," I told Pastor Church shortly after I finished the book he gave me. "There's dope in my dorm, and the cafeteria becomes a discothèque on Saturday nights. It's crazy! Any suggestions?"

Pastor Church recommended that I check out La Sierra College (now La Sierra University) in Riverside, California, about an hour away from CSUN. So I phoned the school, discovered registration day was pending, drove out to Riverside, and met the dean of religion. And because this man "just happened" to know Pastor Church (a mere coincidence?), he immediately wrote a recommendation for my entry into the theology program!

"Can I switch from Cal State Northridge to a Christian college?" I asked my dad as we talked in my dorm room a few days later. After a rather spirited interchange (this was one of the few times we've ever argued), my mystified father finally conceded. "OK," he said, "under one condition. I paid one thousand dollars to get you into this dorm. If you can retrieve my deposit, you can go."

In a flash, I disappeared (this is the closest I've ever come to being raptured), raced down the stairs from the second floor, and rushed to the front desk in the lobby. "Excuse me," I said to an academic-looking woman, "I'm considering changing schools. My dad paid one thousand dollars for my room upstairs. Can we get our money back?"

Looking me over, she blinked, and replied, "Tomorrow is your last day for a refund."

"Praise God!" I shouted, completely unmindful of CSUN protocol. And within a week, I had changed my college major from marketing to ministry. Goodbye statistics and economics! Now I could study the Bible *in school!* And guess what was the required textbook for one of my classes? *The Desire of Ages!* Clearly, God's hand was in this.

At La Sierra, my grades improved dramatically because now I had an exciting purpose in life. For the first time, I knew I wasn't on earth just to dance in discos and gratify every immoral impulse raging inside me. Not anymore. I was here to serve the Man who sacrificed His life for me, to share His love and truth with others, and to form a godly character through His enabling grace. Life had become satisfying and worth living!

After graduating from college, I pastored churches in California, North Dakota, and Kansas. Throughout that entire period, I felt an inner call to share God's Word with a wider audience. This conviction burned inside me; I couldn't shake it. One night I was lying alone on the top bunk inside a friend's RV in Washington State, and rain was pouring onto the roof just inches above my head. "God, if You want me to go out into the world to teach Your Word," I prayed in the midst of thunderous patter, "I'll do it, if You'll open the doors."

Shortly thereafter, I attended a large church event in Indianapolis, Indiana. The year was 1990. Literally tens of thousands of people were there, attending seminars and workshops and just socializing. I found an unoccupied seminar room, slipped inside, switched off the lights, and prayed that God would lead me to someone of experience under whom I could train. Just then a Bible text flashed into my mind repeatedly, "He who walks with wise men will be wise" (Proverbs 13:20). Sensing that the Holy Spirit was speaking to me, I determined then and there to ask one of the best and most experienced evangelists I could find to take me under his wing.

Within an hour, I saw Mark Finley, an internationally known speaker and prophecy expert who has shared the good news of Jesus Christ around the world. I didn't know it at the time (nor did he), but Mark would later replace George Vandeman as speaker and director of the *It Is Written* television program, the very ministry whose TV show resulted in my reading *The Desire of Ages*.

"Hello, Mark. I'm Steve Wohlberg. I'm now pastoring four small churches in North Dakota. Is there any chance you will be teaching a seminar close by in the near future, and can I train under you?"

Mark's answer thrilled me. "I will soon hold a series in Niles, Michigan, and will train fifteen ministers."

"How many do you have now?" I asked anxiously.

"Eight. You can become number nine if the Lord works it out."

Guess what? He did!

After training under Mark Finley and after many other providential events too numerous to mention, in 1993 I was hired by a radio and TV ministry called Amazing Facts to conduct Bible prophecy seminars. My first assignment was to go to New Zealand. Then I went to Indiana and then to Russia with Joe Crews, the founder of the ministry. As this unfolded, I knew that my prayers in the storm in Washington State and in that unoccupied Indianapolis room were being answered. During almost six years of employment with Amazing Facts, God opened door after door for me to share the good news of Jesus Christ, other prophetic truths, and the message of Jesus' soon return in cities across the United States and overseas.

Shortly after our Savior's resurrection, He promised His followers, " 'You shall receive power when the Holy Spirit has come upon you; and you shall be witnesses to Me in Jerusalem, and in all Judea and Samaria, and to the end of the earth' " (Acts 1:8). This happened to me. I stood before audiences with an open Bible and felt "the power of the Holy Spirit" (Romans 15:13) working through me. With my own eyes, I saw God bring light, love, happiness, and hope to thousands.

I saw God at work particularly in Russia, after Soviet Communism collapsed. Our team gave Bibles to those who had never touched a Bible in their entire lives. At the conclusion of a series of gospel meetings in a city called Balakovo, five Russian pastors and I baptized 129 people in a lake while a Russian choir sang on the shore. The last person to be baptized was a very large man who had just been released from prison for killing another man in defense of his friend. After waiting until everyone else had been baptized, he waded out straight to me, and I had the privilege of lowering him into the water in the name of Jesus Christ. Words can't describe the happiness we felt.

Fifty years after returning to heaven, Jesus appeared to His aged disciple John with this definite message: " '*Write* the things which you have seen' " (Revelation 1:19, emphasis added). The result was Revelation, the greatest prophecy book ever written.

Writing was something I never even considered until I joined Amazing Facts. While I've never seen a vision like John did, the urge to write eventually became so strong I literally rolled over in bed one night, got on my knees, and told the Lord, "OK, I'll write! But You must help me."

Now, many books have my name on them, among them *The Antichrist Chronicles, End Time Delusions,* and *Hour of the Witch,* which explores the wildly popular Harry Potter series. I even wrote a book for animal lovers; it's called *Will My Pet Go to Heaven?* A man approached me in the rugged mountains near Malo, Washington, one evening when I was holding a seminar there. "I was giving up drugs, and then my dog died," this tough-looking man said with teary eyes. "If it hadn't been for *Will My Pet Go to Heaven?* I wouldn't have made it. Thanks so much for writing that book." Praise God! These things make life worth living.

It's all pretty amazing. Who would have guessed that this lizard-catching kid from the Hollywood Hills, this aimless secular Jewish teenage druggy, this disco-loving John Travolta wannabe, would become a believer in Jesus Christ, a seminar speaker, and a writer of books about prophecy, Harry Potter, and pets! Heavenly angels must be smiling.

"How did you get into radio?" someone asked me recently.

It started in 1999, in Texas. Somehow, a Los Angeles radio host named Rich Agazino heard about this Jewish Christian who writes about end-time prophecy. "Can I interview you on my show Crosstalk?" Rich asked me by phone.

"Sure!" I said. "Let's go."

This opportunity was great because I didn't have to fly to LA; I could sit in my Texas apartment and hold up my end of the interview via telephone. That show was heard all over Los Angeles.

Amazing! I thought. *Through radio interviews, I can discuss the Bible and the news and be heard by millions of people.* A light went on in my head.

That was just the beginning. Since then, God has opened doors for me to be on more than four hundred radio shows across North America and around the world. Topics have included the Left Behind series, the rapture, Israel, antichrist, Armageddon, the Ten Commandments, the Middle East peace process, Mel Gibson's *Passion* film, Hollywood's impact on culture, September 11, Asia's tsunami, hurricane Katrina, Harry Potter, Wicca witchcraft, the perils of trying to contact the dead, and even the pain people suffer when their dog, cat, or horse dies.

In Texas, a group of us—which included many volunteers—birthed the Texas Media Center to produce TV programs. With God's help and gifts from generous donors, we filmed *Amazing Discoveries, Israel in Prophecy, The Antichrist Chronicles, and Jewish Discoveries in Scripture.* A few years later, thanks to Prophetic Ministries in California, we produced *End Time Delusions, Hour of the Witch,* and *Deadly Delusions About Death and Hell.*

In 2003, the Three Angels Broadcasting Network providentially picked up *Amazing Discoveries.* As of this writing, that series has aired for more than two years and has touched the hearts of people around the world. "*Amazing Discoveries* changed my life," said a twenty-year-old boy who introduced himself to me at a church gathering in Soquel, California. "I'm a Christian because of that series!" To God be the glory!

In a sense, God has brought me full circle. In 1979, He took me *out* of Hollywood, *out* from being an extra, and *out* of television. Yet in the past few years, He has unmistakably moved me back into radio and TV to communicate Bible truth through media to a world enthralled by the same things that captured me in the 1970s. Mick Jagger still blazes his trail, and now Britney Spears and Madonna mesmerize multitudes. But as planet Earth ignorantly rushes toward the "last day" (John 6:39, 40, 44, 54), God has something infinitely better for every one of us than this world's sex, sin, and silliness. That something is a Person. His name is Jesus Christ. *He's still the Desire of ages.*

My sister once told my father, "If Steve hadn't become a Christian, he would probably be dead." She was right. Years after becoming a believer in a crucified and resurrected Messiah, the man who wrote most of the New Testament confessed, "By the grace of God I am what I am" (1 Corinthians 15:10). That's true of me too. I can't do anything truly good without Him. A famous Christian hymn declares, "Nothing in my hands I bring, simply to Thy cross I cling."

I've messed up many times since I first knelt in the dorm. But through God's faithfulness and encouragement, I keep getting up and pressing on. My goal is complete victory over sin through the grace of Jesus Christ (see John 8:11, 34–36; Revelation 2:7). My prayer today is, "Lord, help me to honor You. Take me into Your kingdom at last, and use me to help many others get there."

I'm thankful that many of my family members have become believers in God and His Word. Recently, my father, who is seventy-six years old as I write this, told me by phone, "I've memorized and can recite one hundred and eight Bible texts. It takes about two hours, but it's great!"

I can hardly believe it. God is so good!

Before I end this book, I want to share a bit more about my wife and son. Almost everyone considered me an incorrigible bachelor. But after years of searching for Miss Right, on July 25, 1998, I met Kristin Renee Demarest, the sweetest woman on earth. After a year and a half of dating, I overcame my chronically cold feet and mustered enough courage to say "I do" inside a large church in Sacramento, California. Five years later, Seth came along. (I've told the incredible story of my wife's frightening complications, my unexpected departure to the hospital in the middle of a sermon, and the blessings of Seth's healthy birth in my book *Hour of the Witch,* in a chapter titled "The Motivation: Love's Chamber of Secrets.")

Seth is now fourteen months old. He's already fractured his head on our floor, slammed headlong onto the edge of the hearth in our living room (he actually *chipped* the tile), and bruised himself more times than we can count. But so far, he's survived everything and is healthy, happy, and loads of fun. He smiles, giggles, wrinkles his nose in the funniest way, and laughs a lot. Kristin and I love him so much. The most beautiful sight my eyes have ever seen—other than a baptism and the sight of Kristin in her wedding dress—is little Seth playing peacefully in the sand in our backyard. Parents, you know what I mean. Even though I love sharing God's Word through media, I'm learning that my family comes first. Dads, don't forget this!

Once baby Seth had an awful night, as babies often do. He cried and cried and kept on crying, refusing to be comforted. About 2 A.M., I picked him up and carried him around our house in Paso Robles. I started singing a simple Scripture song based on John 3:16, " 'For God so loved the world, that He gave His only begotten Son, that whoever believes in Him should not perish but have everlasting life.' " As I sang, I felt tremendous love for my baby boy. Then I thought of Jesus crying in Gethsemane and how His Father must have felt seeing Him suffer. Tears welled up in my eyes, and this thought struck home: *Oh God! You gave Your Son to save my son!* Words can't describe my gratitude for Their sacrifice.

In 1988, a devastating earthquake shook Armenia, killing nearly thirty thousand people in four minutes. When the ground stopped rattling, a father thought of his son, whom he had just dropped off at school. "No matter what happens, I'll always be there for you!" he had often promised his boy. So, dodging boulders along cracked streets, he headed to the school as quickly as he could.

When he arrived, he was horrified to find that it was just a pile of rubble. The situation appeared hopeless. But, estimating the location of his son's classroom, this devastated father began digging amidst the ruins.

One hour. Two hours. Four hours.

"It's no use!" other parents cried. "They're all dead."

"My son is here. Will you help me?" the man said, and kept digging.

Eight hours. Twelve hours. Fourteen hours.

"Fires are burning throughout the city—go home!" urged a firefighter.

"My son is here. Will you help me?" the man said, and kept digging.

Eighteen hours. Twenty-two hours. Twenty-six hours.

"There's a curfew. It's dangerous—go home!" barked a police officer.

"My son is here. Will you help me?" the father said again, and kept digging.

Thirty hours. Thirty-three hours . . .

After thirty-six hours, this immovable man pulled a board from the bottom of the large hole he had dug and found a dark cavern formed by the wooden beams of the structure as it collapsed. "Armand, are you there?" he called as he peered into the dusty darkness. "Armand?" he yelled again, and then waited.

What happened next seemed unbelievable. A little boy's voice floated up from the bottom of that death hole. "Dad! Dad! It's me—Armand! I told the other kids not to worry because I knew that if you were alive, you would come. [Thirteen others had survived too.] I remembered your promise, 'I'll always be there for you!' "

Dear reader, I don't know what is happening in your life right now. Maybe it seems that everything is collapsing all around you, just like that school building crumbled in Armenia. Life can be so cruel. Do you feel trapped beneath the ground, in the darkest of caves, with no light? Maybe you're wondering if anyone cares; if there's any hope.

Yes, there's Someone who cares. There is hope! Whether or not you believe it, know it, or feel it, there is Someone digging to reach you, just like that father dug for his son. That Someone is Jesus Christ, your Savior. He knows all about Lucifer's rebellion, about planet Earth's detour, about your problems, disappointments, heartaches, and pain. He knows everything. Two thousand years ago, He left heaven for you, became the Bethlehem Baby, lived a perfect life, told stories, healed the sick, endured opposition, suffered in Gethsemane, experienced betrayal, beatings, sharp nails, splintery wood, and—more painful than anything else—the hiding of His Father's face, which pierced His heart in ways we'll never know. He did it for you. He loves you. He paid the full price for your sins. And on the third day, He rose from the dead.

At this very moment, Jesus Christ is digging—removing barriers and calling your name. He won't give up, because you are His child. *Will you answer His call,* forsake your sins, and believe in what He has already accomplished for you by His death and resurrection? If you haven't already done so, why not pray a prayer just as I did in my dorm room at CSUN? If you don't know what to say, use my prayer. Say something like: "Dear God, I believe that Jesus Christ is Your Son, that He died for me on the cross and rose again. I've done a lot of bad things. I'm not worthy. But if You still want me, if You'll take me, please forgive me and save me from my sins. In Jesus' name, amen."

You don't have to worry about whether God will hear or answer your prayer. He will for sure. He has promised, "No matter what, I'll always be there for you!" (see Hebrews 13:5). He rescued me. He can rescue you!

---

1. Adapted from a sermon titled "Arise, Sir Knight," attributed to Dr. James Allen Francis and preached at the First Baptist Church of Los Angeles on July 11, 1926.

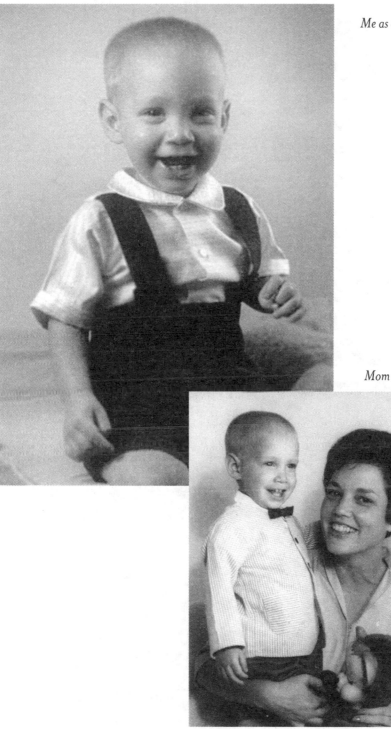

Me as a toddler.

Mom and me.

*My brother, Mike, and
my sister, Cathy, with
me. I'm in the middle.*

Mike, Mom, and me.

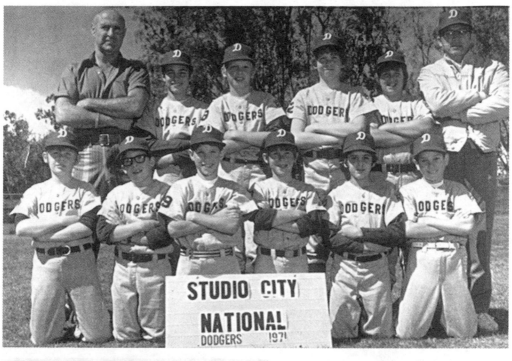

Little League baseball: Dad's at the upper left, Mike's at the lower right, and I'm kneeling above the word STUDIO.

Cathy, Mike, and me—all dressed up.

My family at Mike's bar mitzvah.

Mike and me out fishing.

Before I knew Jesus.

Kristin Demarest and I were married April 9, 2000, in Sacramento, California.

Our son, Seth, on his first birthday. (Do you think he looks like me?!)

Seth on my shoulders as we're about to go for a walk.

The family God has blessed me with.

Dad came when I was ordained to the gospel ministry in North Dakota in June 1991.

God has given me the privilege of preaching the gospel in many places—in this photo, I'm in Murom, Russia, and Andre Dyman is translating for me.